MANAGING CORPORATE WEALTH

MANAGING CORPORATE WEALTH

The Operation of a Comprehensive Financial Goals System

Gordon Donaldson

Graduate School of Business Administration
Harvard University

with the editorial assistance of
Nan Dundes Stone

PRAEGER

PRAEGER SPECIAL STUDIES • PRAEGER SCIENTIFIC

New York • Philadelphia • Eastbourne, UK
Toronto • Hong Kong • Tokyo • Sydney

Library of Congress Cataloging in Publication Data

Donaldson, Gordon, 1922–

    Managing corporate wealth.

    Bibliography: p.
    Includes index.
    1. Corporations – United States – Finance. I. Stone,
Nan Dundes. II. Title.
HG4061.D58 1984   658.1'5   84–4779
ISBN 0–03–063414–8
ISBN 0–03–063416–4 (pbk.)

Published in 1984 by Praeger Publishers
CBS Educational and Professional Publishing,
a Division of CBS Inc.
521 Fifth Avenue, New York, NY 10175 USA

56789 052 9876543

Printed in the United States of America
on acid-free paper

Acknowledgments

E very author owes a debt of gratitude to those who have broken the ground before him or her. Their ideas influence one's own to an extent which cannot be accurately or objectively assessed. However, these debts are particularly difficult to repay when the subject has received thoughtful attention for a century or more—as this one has. Under those circumstances even the best bibliographies are likely to be partial because the relevant literature is so extensive. That my bibliography necessarily falls into this category will be obvious, even though it also reflects my best efforts to acknowledge all such debts.

My indebtedness to the top executives who allowed their companies to participate in this study is equally difficult to acknowledge directly, because they must remain anonymous. Yet the fact remains that this study could not have gone forward without their willingness to risk giving us open access to their records and personnel. I am grateful for the unqualified cooperation afforded us, and I deeply appreciate the confidence these corporate leaders have placed in my ability to judge the facts as I saw them.

The Division of Research of the Harvard Business School was as generous in supporting this project as our subjects were in opening their corporate records. In addition to considerable financial support over several years, two of its directors, Richard Rosenbloom and Raymond Corey, have given me encouragement and counsel, as have members of their staff. Their contributions were critical in sustaining the effort required to bring the book to publication.

Friends and colleagues at the Harvard Business School and the University's Department of Economics have been involved in this project at many steps along the way. Chief among them are John McArthur and Jay Lorsch, who shared in designing the broad research project on which this study rests. Those early conversations contributed significantly to the shape of this final work, as did the many discussions with Jay that led to our coauthored work, *Decision Making at the Top: The Shaping of Strategic Direction*. This book has gained significantly from that close and continuous interaction, as have I. In addition, I acknowledge gratefully the contributions and constructive criticism given me by Richard Caves, William Fruhan, Carl Kester, James Medoff, David Mullins, Malcolm Salter, and Michael Spence. The manuscript benefited substantially from their detailed comments, though the final responsibility for its contents remains my own.

The actual research was conducted with the help of James Singer and Carl Kester. Jim worked on the project during its early data-gathering days, and Carl was involved at every stage of the research. Both contributed dedication and creativity for which I am very grateful. I am likewise indebted to Professor Norman Josephy for his help in preparing the computer tables and graphs found in Appendix A. Special thanks also are due to Janet Norman, my secretary, who managed the lengthy process of manuscript production with remarkable patience and good humor.

Finally I wish to acknowledge the invaluable editorial help I have received from Nan Stone. She has been closely involved in reworking the early drafts to improve the clarity and cogency of the ideas. The result is a vastly improved final draft.

Contents

1

An Introduction to Managing Corporate Wealth

Among top management's responsibilities the selection of key financial goals figures prominently. Yet the formulation of these goals and the way in which they discipline management's use of financial resources have not been sufficiently explored. In particular there have been few attempts to describe in detail the management of corporate wealth from the inside, as it is practiced on a day-to-day basis, in the open-ended and uncertain flow of events. This book attempts to do just that. Comparisons, generalizations, and interpretations enter in, where appropriate, but its guiding principle has been to record observed realities as carefully and as objectively as possible, without the filters created by prior expectations and assumptions.

The research study on which this book is based examined a dozen mature industrial firms over a decade or more of their recent history. Undertaken jointly with Professor Jay Lorsch of the Harvard Business School, the project brought together authors with specialties in organizational behavior and corporate finance. Its primary findings, published in *Decision Making at the Top: The Shaping of Strategic Direction*, were more broadly focused than those presented here.[1] In the initial study the economic and financial dimensions of corporate management were appropriately seen as part of the larger framework of organizational constraints that define the discretionary space within which corporate leadership is exercised. In this book those dimensions are brought onto center stage.

Of all the resource bases on which corporate activity is constructed, financial resources are the most readily quantified. As a result, they are a uniquely productive source on two counts. First, they allow us to track the process by which specific financial goals are transformed into particular courses of action; second, they allow us to evaluate the results of those choices by measuring corporate performance against management's intent. Thus this book's specialized focus illuminates top management's practice in closer detail than was possible in *Decision Making at the Top*. And yet, its objective findings fully support the more general observations found in that initial volume. Whether one concentrates on psychological and organizational considerations or on economic and financial factors, the moral remains the same: Even at the highest level, management's options are limited. Discretionary space does exist, and it can be increased through well-chosen corporate strategies, as we shall see. But overall, the weight of the evidence falls on the relatively narrow boundaries within which management chooses its financial goals and sets its investment priorities.

Under such circumscribed conditions, the value of considered choices is self-evident. Consequently, two audiences should be particularly interested in this study's findings. One is the managerial audience, composed of those who practice—or are affected by—the financial planning and resource allocation process. The other is the academic audience, composed of students and observers of business organization and management practice.

For the first group, particularly the financial managers, this book provides a method for interpreting personal experience and a framework for reevaluating individual practice. If the sample is as representative as we believe, the state-of-the-art financial planning described here will usefully confirm—or challenge—the reader's current thinking and methods. At the same time, nonfinancial senior managers can draw on its observations to better understand and interpret financial decisions that touch on their own spheres of influence as well as the corporate strategies that underlie them.

Academic readers should also profit from the hands-on approach followed in this study because it opens a perspective on corporate financial management rarely seen in the existing literature. That literature is vast; but, for the most part, it is also theoretical. Its visions of corporate motivation and intent begin with classical concepts of free enterprise and private property, legal and regulatory precedents, or market theory; and they describe the business world as it ought to be. In contrast, this study attempts to describe the world as it is, and it adopts the perspective of the individual manager—an appropriate starting point even for those who wish to bring "is" and "ought" together.

Managing Corporate Wealth: Defining Relevant Terms

Although some people consider the accumulation of wealth a corporation's ultimate purpose while others think it a means to an end, all would agree it is essential, if the company is to pursue its business mission successfully. However, no such unanimity extends to the term corporate wealth. On the contrary, both the form and the magnitude of the entity specified by that term reflect the purpose and point of view of the respondent. Thus the corporation's wealth at any particular moment in time means one thing to a stockholder who wishes to liquidate his or her investment, another to a creditor considering a loan, and still another to a manager who hopes to build a new plant.

In keeping with its central purpose, this book considers corporate wealth from a managerial perspective (that is, as it supports the firm's competitive activity in its various product-market initiatives). Therefore, it defines corporate wealth in terms of *the aggregate purchasing power available to management for strategic purposes during any given planning period*. As we shall see, this wealth consists of the stocks and flows of cash or cash equivalents (primarily credit) that management can use at its discretion to implement decisions involving the control of goods and services. However, its aggregate is often difficult to measure because it is affected by three separate variables: quantity, quality (or conditions of availability), and timing. Among other things, this means that traditional balance sheet footings often mismeasure actual stocks and flows of corporate wealth. For example, items that appear as liabilities (such as lines of credit or long-term debt capacity) may actually represent potential purchasing power, whereas cash balances or other liquid assets may be unavailable for strategic purposes because they have already been assigned to other uses (e.g., as reserves against seasonal variations in working capital).

Standard financial reporting conventions intensify these problems, in large part because they reflect past values rather than current or prospective purchasing power. For example, however realistic the dollar value assigned to an oil refinery in active use, it is a meaningless number to a financial planner searching for funds to expand the facility (except in the limited sense of its possible relation to unused debt capacity). Therefore, familiar balance sheet assets tend to measure funds that are unavailable for future use rather than those that are or will be at management's command. Similar problems arise if a traditional income statement is used to measure the flows of discretionary purchasing power accessible to corporate management. Following the same accounting conventions which apply to the balance sheet, the income statement measures changes in book value assigned to a particular reporting period rather than the release of liquid funds. Thus the information customarily provided by standard financial reports requires substantial transformation to produce appropriate data for the actual management of corporate wealth.

What is meant by management in this context is straightforward: it denotes *the ability to direct the inflow and outflow of discretionary funds in accordance with an existing or future corporate strategy.* Ironically, in the very short term few opportunities for such management exist. This situation holds true because virtually all the company's inflows will have been committed by prior decisions to the funding of contracts that have now become essentially unbreakable. Because these legal obligations, industry practices, internal budget approvals, and strategic priorities capture most of the company's day-to-day spending, corporate cash flows include little, if any, of consumers' impulse buying. However, commitments also have their time limits and as the planning period lengthens, the fraction of available funds flows representing true discretionary income increases. Thus management in the sense used here becomes a critical aspect of the financial planning process, which focuses on identifying future discretionary funds and relating them to the range of current decisions and actions that could affect their magnitude and commit their use.

The primary administrative tool in this process is the five-year financial plan, and it therefore stands first among this study's objective data. As distinguished from one-year operating and capital budgets and monthly, weekly, or daily cash projections, the five-year plan reflects an arbitrary time line reaching beyond most of the financial commitments made by past decisions and actions. Its expenditures will always include a certain number of legal entitlements (such as long-term bond interest or lease and production payments); but these plans are possible precisely because most of a company's expenses five years out are relatively unpredictable—contradictory as that may seem. In this sense financial planning represents the extrapolation of existing strategic momentum, a range of assumptions about the environment, and the identification of critical choices in the immediate future which will affect the outcome.

Long-range (five-year) corporate plans are typically comprehensive documents. Among the information customarily included in the plan of a large-scale enterprise are: a statement of business mission (or the broad boundaries of corporate activity); management's objectives for its shareholders, consumers, employees, and society at large; specific goals for the planning period (including numerical targets affecting the stocks and flows of financial resources); corporate and product-market strategies (both general and specific); outlines for resource allocations consistent with corporate portfolio strategy; and working assumptions about the political, economic, and competitive environment. In addition, the plan will contain detailed projections on a year-to-year basis for sales and earnings by product line, balance sheets, and cash or funds flows. Predicated on the assumption that management's objectives will be successfully accomplished, these statements attest to the fact that all potential conflicts and inconsistencies have been identified and reconciled, at least for the purposes of the plan, promising the continuation of a solvent, independent, and profitable enterprise.

As this summary indicates, the corporate long-range plan deals with more than the custody and management of corporate financial wealth, narrowly defined. Consequently, it provides both a point of entry into the decision-making process and an inside view of the factors and forces that will ultimately determine the accumulation and distribution of the company's wealth. From this latter perspective, the major concerns that characterize the management of wealth are the nature and limits of the resource base to be employed in the formal business plan; the choice of particular product markets within which the company will fulfill its business mission; targeted operation levels within each product market (including expenditures and anticipated cash generation); existing and anticipated commitments for external funds; and the stock of funds on reserve (internally and externally), at each point of the planning cycle.

Perhaps surprisingly, neither earnings nor equity values appear in this list of major concerns. However, these omissions are justified, given the real-world limits on management's authority and responsibility. For example, while it is true that management is held accountable for corporate earnings, it is less clear that those earnings are managed in the same sense that funds are managed. Obviously top management dedicates a great deal of attention to matters related to the generation of earnings. But the cause-and-effect relationship is often obscure, and the final tally will depend on many factors including competitive and economic conditions beyond management's control.

Even greater uncertainties exist in terms of management's responsibility for equity values or stockholder wealth. Once again, there is no denying that equity values are a serious concern among top management, nor that it is happy to take the credit if the company's stock outperforms the market or the industry. But the internal planning process does not pretend that equity value is, or can be, managed or controlled. Managers control resources and thereby have an impact on earnings and corporate wealth for which they can be held accountable. But the indices monitored by external investors, the relative importance attached to each, and the multiplier applied by the market to earnings and assets are all beyond management's control. Consequently, the planning documents reviewed in this study focused, appropriately, on funds flows, and they stopped at the border of management responsibility with earnings or earnings per share. None referred to equity values or market variables, which were left for outside parties to determine. Like Olympic competitors, the managers were prepared to do their best and wait for the judges to evaluate their performance against that of their competitors.

The Research Design

The evidence on which this study rests was obtained through a comprehensive review of individual firms' and managers' experiences. Such a research design has negative consequences as well as positive ones. It severely limits the number of observations or research sites that can be included within a reasonable period of time, and its eclectic approach to evidence (where the salient issues are relevance and inclusiveness rather than methodological compatibility) tends to diminish strict comparability across the research sample. Nevertheless, these weaknesses seem sufficiently offset by the greater descriptive detail possible with an individualized approach, particularly when care is taken to develop all evidence as fully as possible and to identify its nature and origin so that the reader will have some degree of independence in interpreting the study's conclusions.

Following confirmation by a chief executive of his organization's willingness to participate in the study, the research team met with a member of top management to agree on the data to be made available. Given the number of contexts in which management customarily discusses its financial goals, it is inevitable that the tone and content of those discussions will be affected by the nature of the audience. In particular, management must assume that public statements will be available to all parties, including some who might use the information to the company's disadvantage. Hence, intentionally or not, these statements at times convey different (or even conflicting) impressions from those found in private documents, if only so that the company's competitors will not be privy to its goals and strategies. To minimize deliberate or inadvertent distortion of the evidence, therefore, this study focused on the private record, where management spoke directly to management, in the context of the day-to-day actions its goals were intended to shape. Certain public documents (notably speeches and reports to analysts) have been used as secondary sources when available, but the integrity of the study rests upon the internal records that constitute its primary source of evidence.

Documents available to us included annual planning reports, budgeting manuals, project analyses, conference records, interoffice reports and memos, speeches, and special studies—all of which allowed us to capture management's thinking and intent, free of retrospective filters. In addition, we examined detailed records of financial and corporate performance ordinarily reserved for management's use, as well as facts and interpretive information on the company, its competitors, and the firm's economic environment. Thus these documents allowed us to test management's accuracy and consistency as we compared them over an extended period of time.

An extensive series of interviews supplemented each company's written documents. We met with financial, planning, and operating executives who constituted the top management team. We spoke with lower-level divisional managers who were subject to the discipline of the planning and goal-setting process. We also spoke with past and present chief executives and, when relevant, with the company's principal shareholders. To ensure a complete and accurate record, two interviewers were usually present at each session. However, we met with each respondent individually, whenever possible, so that remembered plans and events could be cross-checked for accuracy and detail from several participants' perspectives.

The framework for these interviews was provided by corporate records, which suggested topics where further insight and information were necessary. Once begun, however, the sessions were largely nondirective, as befit the temperaments of the successful executives involved and our own desire to minimize bias in their responses. Wide ranging and open ended, these discussions often served the additional purpose of identifying new source documents unknown to others or forgotten by them, which could add to the factual base.

When all the documents and interview notes had been collected, data sheets covering ten or more years of company experience were prepared. These sheets contained the following information:

- Constituency profiles on principal shareholders, principal lenders, top management team members, and principal product lines, primary competitors, and relative market shares.

- Major public and private external financings.

- The performance record of the company's debt and equity securities in the public capital market.

- Events in the capital and product markets that reflected significant discontinuities in the corporate environment.

- Principal elements of the corporate and financial goals systems.

- The company's performance against its goals broken down by income-stream segments.

- Executive compensation system and formulae.

- Corporate peer group comparisons, as available.

- Major discretionary expenditures broken down by primary corporate income-stream segments.

- Capital expenditure guidelines and numerical standards.

- Detailed case histories of two or more major strategic investment decisions.

- A general financial record of overall performance.

Interpreting such a diverse body of data is a challenging task. Complex and unusually researcher dependent, it mixes facts and opinions, current affairs and ancient history, interested and disinterested parties and views. Consequently, the general principle governing the study has been the need for multiple evidentiary sources on any given issue. Documentary and interview data must agree, so that facts represent the absence of significant contradiction among the sources. In addition, a policy of full disclosure has been applied to all the major issues so that the reader will have a reasonable opportunity to make an independent judgment. When conclusions are uncertain or qualified, the study makes that known.

A Trial Run

Before the major research effort was undertaken, the study's methods and questions were tested in a pilot study lasting more than a year. A brief description of this trial run follows, to give the reader an integrated perspective on the data-collection process and a flavor of the field research.

In this instance the company was initially approached through its chief financial officer who secured the chief executive's approval. The

CFO then assigned a senior member of his staff to assist in assembling documents and arranging interviews. Our liaison's long experience and broad company contacts proved valuable, as did the company's practice of holding periodic strategy conferences at which top executives presented papers on critical issues and corporate goals. The proceedings of these top management conferences supplemented the eleven years of corporate records which were at our disposal. They also provided insights into management's decision-making process—as did the opportunity to participate in one such conference, held shortly after research had begun.

After an initial document search and the identification of certain key strategic investment decisions, gaps in the data were noted for further documentation and an interview schedule was set up. These interviews involved a long list of participants, as we spoke with each member of the top management team, with the officers responsible for the major corporate divisions, with their financial officers, with selected subordinate operating executives, and with managers in charge of critical overseas divisions. Some of the latter interviews could be arranged while the managers visited the head office. But a special trip was made to England and the Continent to talk with the key personnel in the dominant European division. The final interview, with the chief executive officer, took place after the data search had been completed.

The results of the pilot study were particularly rewarding. Not all company studies proved to be this detailed at the interview stage, nor were all companies as rich in explanatory documents. Nevertheless, this experience established the validity of the research questions with which the study had begun. As the other research sample companies were approached, we continued to ask:

• What financial goals were formulated by top management and communicated to the management team over the decade or more preceding the date of the study?

• How did these goals originate, and why did they assume their specific numerical values?

• What were the key elements among the company's financial goals and how did they relate to one another?

• How and why did the company's financial goals change over time, and which conditions promoted stability or instability?

• What was the nature of the financial resource allocation process, and how did it relate to the company's financial goals?

The Research Sample

The management process whereby financial goals are formulated, administered, and modified is difficult to observe under the best circumstances. Thus the decision to restrict the research sample to large and mature corporations reflects the fact that such companies are most likely to make this process explicit. Formal written records are essential when many people at multiple levels throughout an organization are involved in decision making and implementation. Geographic dispersal provides a similarly strong incentive for formal records, while multinational operations make the articulation of implicit assumptions and values a virtual necessity if economic, social, political, and cultural differences are to be overcome successfully. In keeping with these guidelines, therefore, every company in the sample was large enough to fall within the top half of the *Fortune* 500 list of industrial companies (i.e., sales volume in excess of $1 billion and assets in excess of $600 million). In addition, a large majority had extensive international activities, although all were owned and managed from a U.S. base.

Other considerations led to further restrictions on the sample. Chief among them was the decision to exclude regulated companies to avoid the distortion in management's priorities that inevitably occurs when a government agency enters into the free market process. No business is entirely free of regulatory influence, of course. But government involvement in pricing, investment, or rate of return would impinge on the very heart of this study, in ways that would make management's independent judgments impossible to identify. We also chose to limit the sample to industrial companies, because they share traditions for reporting and evaluating results and because they are reasonably comparable in their asset, liability, and income-statement characteristics. However, to avoid an unintentional industry bias and to better assure confidentiality to the participating companies, we opted for wide diversity among industries. Accordingly, no two companies in the sample come from the same industry.

Lastly, issues of access and confidentiality played an important part in the selection process. To ensure full disclosure no study was undertaken unless the company agreed to give the research team unrestricted access to its documents and management personnel, past and present. In return, all information was to be held in confidence. Nothing would be said to identify a company or its personnel, and all relevant manuscript sections were to be submitted to the company for review. These agreements have been honored on both sides. Each company exercised its right to review the text; none sought modifications or deletions.

Once these guidelines were in place, twelve major industrial firms were chosen for the core sample, although the authors' experience with other companies entered into the initial research design. This number was small enough to allow an intensive investigation of each company during the two- to three-year period planned for the research. It was also large enough to diminish the possibility that the unique experience of one company or one set of managers would dominate the findings.

As should be clear, the sample is not intended to represent a statistically defined population or segment of business enterprise. For those concerned with this issue it can only be said that in-depth analysis of confidential data and statistical objectivity are difficult, if not impossible, to reconcile. However, every effort has been made to keep the data base and the analysis free from obvious bias. In the end, if the most that can be asserted is a strong hypothesis about real-world behavior, the chief purpose of the study will have been met.

A Preview of the Findings

Chapter 2 discusses financial goals from a managerial perspective. Accordingly, it begins with the concept of business or corporate mission, the unique identity that defines an enterprise in its management's eyes. Some such statement commonly introduces a company's current long-range plan. In addition, its details define specific business activities and thereby demonstrate the need for multiple financial goals to satisfy the corporate partners on whom the mission depends: shareholders, employees, customers, suppliers, and host communities. However, these financial goals are also strongly influenced by management's desire for organizational survival, independence, self-sufficiency, and personal fulfillment. As a result their organizing principle is found in the maximization of corporate wealth (as distinct from shareholder wealth) because it is the quality and quantity of the financial and human resources under management's control that actually support the business mission. To the extent that specific financial goals discipline organizational activity and influence the company's future, they do so through their impact on the inflow and outflow of funds (and therefore corporate wealth).

Chapter 3 describes in detail the individual financial goals, found in varying forms and combinations in every corporation, that have an important impact on the flow of funds. With few exceptions these goals have one overriding objective: funding the established product-market positions which are the mainstay of current corporate earnings. Therefore, on the demand side management's primary emphasis falls on the growth rate of sales and the investment necessary to maintain or improve the company's competitive position in each major market. Among the sample companies this tended to mean that industry growth rates acted as a floor for corporate objectives, because the managers' competitive instincts were reinforced by the widely shared conviction that market share held the key to profitability. Beyond this, above-average growth rates were also fostered by top management's interest in creating an organizational environment in which expanding opportunities, upward mobility, and superior rewards would attract and hold talented managerial and technical personnel.

Goals related to new investment necessarily require complementary funding-related goals. Therefore management's funding strategy for established product markets essential to corporate survival and independence tended to focus on *assured* sources of funds. Experience had taught the managers to mistrust external sources that they could neither predict nor control. In response, they made financial self-sufficiency the central tenet in their financial planning so that the timing, magnitude, and form of strategically critical investments remained theirs to decide. In practical terms this meant that they relied on internally generated equity funds (or retained earnings), coupled with debt conservatively defined to assure an arm's length debtor-creditor relationship. Dominant supply-related goals were limited to the target return on investment, the dividend payout (or earnings retention) policy, and the debt-equity ratio, while supplemental external equity funding was reserved primarily for new product-line initiatives.

In developing the concept of an integrated financial goals system, Chapter 4 builds on the preceding chapter's discussion of funds-flow goals in a capital market that is essentially private, finite, and internal. This system recognizes the inherent necessity for balance between key demand-related and supply-related goals. In fact, once management has chosen to express its financial goals as ratios or rates of change in funds flows it can be represented by an algebraic equation or graph. Thus it becomes apparent that financial goals cannot be set in isolation and that a change in one goal must be accompanied by compensating changes elsewhere in the system. In addition, the chapter presents data for all twelve companies so that the reader can compare goals systems, test for internal consistency, and measure performance against targets for the ten-year period reviewed.

Having described at length the key financial goals that discipline long-range financial planning in industrial corporations, our focus shifts in Chapter 5 to the forces that cause those goals to change over time. Four stand out: a major change in a constituency, a radical shift in management's expectations, a significant performance gap, and a persistent funding gap. Because each of these events is commonly found among a typical corporation's experiences, it is not surprising that financial goals systems are often under pressure and undergo periodic revision. However, as long-range financial goals must also be relatively stable to fulfill their disciplinary function, management must be alert to these forces of change.

Why significant constituency changes promote revised financial goals should be readily apparent. As previously noted, the enterprise draws essential resources from its product market, capital market, and organization, and its management acknowledges these contributions in choosing its financial goals. Therefore a company's financial goals must change, if and as its constituencies change in important and lasting ways. Changes in management's expectations about the company or its external environment also lead to goal revisions, because financial goals must be realistically related to the world as it is—or is likely to be in the foreseeable future. Indeed, unless management's goals are credible and provide a continuing challenge for those who live under them, they cannot serve their primary function. Thus a persistent record of under- or overachievement must be acknowledged by more realistic targets, while persistent funding gaps must be met by more aggressive growth objectives (in the case of substantial surpluses) or more aggressive return on investment goals (in the case of deficits).

Financial goals reveal their power most meaningfully through their influence on resource allocations. Chapter 6 describes this process in detail, drawing on data from the research study to demonstrate the links between financial goals and management's primary strategic investment choices. In so doing, the discussion departs from conventional methodology, which ranks investment projects on the basis of discounted cash-flow analyses. Instead it divides management's strategic investment decisions into funding strategies, which define the total amount of discretionary spending, year by year; competitive strategies, which allocate resources among the company's major product markets; and business strategies, which determine the product markets in which the firm will compete.

Of these basic strategic-investment decisions, the last is the most critical because it represents management's long-term corporate commitment to the product markets on which the company's survival ultimately depends. Thus it has the most profound significance for the financial goals system. In keeping with that status, Chapter 6 describes three case studies at length, indicating how management made its investment choices and how these choices influenced—and were influenced by—existing corporate financial goals.

The book's remaining chapters focus on what the study's findings mean for the practicing manager. Chapter 7 discusses corporate goal setting and its disciplinary effects in the short term, when corporate constituencies are essentially fixed. Predictably, management has little room to set an independent course under these circumstances, because its critical goals have already been defined by existing product markets, together with its goals for capital and human resources. However, managers can profitably analyze and interpret their recent corporate experience by tracking performance against goals on a grid derived from the self-sustaining growth equation. In addition, the chapter illustrates the boundaries on management's choice of goals and differentiates between corporate and divisional or strategic business unit goals in terms of their relationship to constituent interests. As the reader will see, investment strategies appropriate for the corporation as a whole may be inappropriate for particular product markets given their individual life-cycle stages. Finally, the links between various executive compensation schemes and the principal components of the goals system are explored to emphasize their mutual concern with maximizing corporate wealth.

A long-term perspective emerges in Chapter 8, which discusses strategies for managerial independence in the goal-setting process. As we shall see, to escape the constraints imposed by its market constituencies—and therefore change the components of its financial goals system—management must change the constituencies themselves by finding new product markets, new investors, and/or new manpower with different skills and talents. These searches are not always successful, and the process itself is usually uncertain and slow, with an appropriate time frame set by the incumbent chief executive's term of office.

Product-market diversification figures most prominently among these strategies because the replacement of maturing revenue streams by new and more vigorous market opportunities is seen as vital to long-term organizational survival. Data from the research study demonstrate a decade of managerial efforts to achieve greater diversification as well as a willingness to use external equity funding in the process. However, the evidence also indicates that positive results are more often measured in decades than in years. Further, we conclude that management's ability to achieve true independence is limited because in its struggle to escape the restrictions of one product (or capital) market, it necessarily finds itself the captive of another. Neither management nor the corporation can ever function alone.

The relevance and usefulness of the financial goals system described in this study go beyond the self-interest of individual managers or corporations. Its relevance reflects the fact that any organization, public or private, profit-making or nonprofit, will evolve a set of demand-related and supply-related financial goals if it is committed to performing an economic function and operates with limited resources. Its usefulness is similarly far-reaching in that it efficiently serves society's economic needs— needs that include the organizational capacity and managerial talent required to administer large-scale economic activities successfully.

Notes

1. Gordon Donaldson and Jay W. Lorsch, *Decision Making at the Top: The Shaping of Strategic Direction* (New York: Basic Books, 1983).

2

Achieving the Corporate Mission

Defining the Business Mission

The development of a strong managerial and organizational esprit de corps depends upon shared convictions about a company's worth and unique abilities: what we do and how we do it. The identity that grows out of these convictions varies from company to company, of course. In some companies corporate identity is defined by the particular products the business manufactures or the services it provides. In others it refers to special marketing or production or financial expertise. Still others think first about superiority in scientific, technological, or managerial skills, or territories defined by geographic, social, or political boundaries.

The term often used by top management to refer to organizational identity is *business mission*. Statements of business mission were common among the companies included in the study. For the most part these statements defined organizational fit by identifying the economic or business activities in which the firm's full resources could be optimally employed at the present time and in the future. Thus they indicated the specific areas in which the company's real competitive advantage was thought to lie. By inference therefore, they also suggested the activities that were inappropriate for the firm, the areas that lay outside its particular business competence. As one management aptly said about its mission, we must "do better what we do best."

The origins and rationale of the companies' individual business missions have been discussed elsewhere.[1] Nevertheless, it bears repeating

17

that these missions provide a critical frame of reference for individual managements as they allocate resources and direct the flow of corporate wealth. Private and public purposes may require that these statements be couched in general terms (to allow for an orderly evolution in the firm's business activities, for example, or to avoid giving away competitive strategies). But the members of the top management team understand and accept the fact that it is their business mission that directs them to specific product markets as they choose the areas in which they will compete.

An example will demonstrate the way in which this sense of direction comes about. The following paragraph is taken from the corporate mission statement of a large and very successful consumer-goods enterprise. The statement was included in the company's confidential planning documents and it represents management's private communication with its organization:

> As a major corporation enjoying the rights and responsibilities of the competitive enterprise system [Company Name's] existence and success depend upon the competitive excellence, value, and satisfaction it continually provides consumers through its goods and services. Serving the wants and needs of the consumer by providing real customer value is the objective which guides everyday decisions and is fully consistent with and best assures fulfillment of our obligations to shareholders, to employees, and to society.

A skeptical reader could conclude that this mission cannot constrain nor discipline management's choices. Because it is stated so abstractly it leaves the managers free to do anything they wish. And yet, let us assume that management means what it says, especially when it is speaking privately as it is here. Note the mission's primary emphasis on the consumer as the focus of organizational effort, on competitive excellence, and on responsibilities as well as rights as the guide to "everyday decisions." Note, too, the acknowledged obligations to "shareholders, employees, and society." This statement is clearly a declaration of interdependence, of multiple responsibilities to multiple constituencies, bound together by the goal of competitive excellence in every product market the company serves. It is a statement of the firm as a social institution.

Subsequent paragraphs continue to speak in general terms, as they refer to the individual objectives management expects to accomplish for each of its four primary constituencies. However, abstractions soon give way to particulars in the planning document for which the mission statement provides a preface. Intimate operational details appear on the second page, and details occupy the balance of the plan's fifty-six pages, where all generalities are stripped away. Nevertheless, in moving from the general to the specific, the reader is still made aware of management's firm intention to achieve its goals on the basis of "demonstrated skills in marketing consumer products." The phrase indicates clearly the managers' conviction about their firm's existing proprietary advantage; it also suggests the direction for its future development. Thus it links the operating plan closely to the prefatory mission statement.

Before turning to the details which implement the company's corporate mission on a product market by product-market basis, the strategic plan lays out the specific goals management has chosen to fulfill the company's "obligations to shareholders, employers, consumers, and society." Here we find more than a dozen quantitative goals which include regular dividend increases for shareholders, a minimum ratio of earnings coverage for bond-interest obligations, a sustained corporate growth rate for employees seeking job security and upward mobility, and substantial new investment in established product markets to keep pace with customers' needs and preferences. Significantly, the paragraph that introduces the company's specific financial goals contains the following statement: "[The targets] will be achieved *solely* from present business areas and new business areas entered through internal development. Acquisitions made during the planning period will normally add to or strengthen the stated targets" (company's emphasis). In other words, acquisitions were the frosting on a cake made up of established product markets. The company's true business mission was seen to lie in the application of its stated goals to the specific competitive opportunities within existing lines of business—paper clips or toasters or baking soda.

The detailed plan then proceeds to stake out the territory to be taken against established competition by each strategic business unit. Targets are set for market penetration (and the date by which it is to be achieved), for the growth rate in sales and earnings, for necessary additions to productive capacity, and for new products. The lofty ideals of the opening paragraphs, which speak of the "rights and responsibilities of the competitive enterprise system," ultimately take shape in the down-to-earth, even grubby, details of the competitive struggle for individual consumers' hearts, minds, and pocketbooks.

A company's established product-market mix evolves over time—gradually, and often intermittently. Typically the time frame for significant change is set by decades rather than years. However, once a product market has become firmly established within the organizational mix, it tends to gather its own momentum and develop an instinct for self-preservation. Two explanations for this phenomenon suggest themselves. The first considers the complex, time-consuming process of establishing and maintaining a major product-market position against determined and able competition and the equally complex and time-consuming process of withdrawing in an orderly, wealth-conserving manner. The second, equally important, reflects the strength of established beliefs, expectations, and preferences within an organization in which most of the top managers have spent their working lives. These beliefs evolve, but at a glacierlike pace.

Financially and emotionally invested in their existing product markets, most professional managers do not fit the popular image of the corporate cherry-picker, quickly discarding old businesses or poor acquisitions. Such behavior is more characteristic of a few highly visible masters of merger and acquisition than it is of professional management's rank and file. The latter know that sustainable competitive positions require long and continuous nurturing, and they are reluctant to abandon established positions for the uncertainty of new ventures. Moreover, they tend to view managements that move in and out of diverse product markets and shun industry classification with suspicion. From their perspective, the conglomerate managers' regard for financial performance and perceived shareholder satisfaction misstates management's first priority: customer satisfaction and loyalty.

The Motives Behind the Mission

As previously indicated, this study examines the management of corporate wealth from an internal perspective. It is concerned with the organization's view rather than that of the partners outside the firm whose legal claims entitle them to share in its success. Therefore the question of underlying motives is directed at top management: What leads to its unique concept of the business mission?

Because the question deals with the inner springs of human motivation, it may appear presumptuous to attempt a categoric statement about what makes Sammy run. However, careful observation suggests that common elements are present in top managers' thoughts about their firms and corporate goals. As the managers strive to promote their business missions, they are strongly influenced by motives they share with their peers in other companies.[2]

The first and most fundamental of these motives is survival: the long-term health and vitality of the organization as an effective and influential corporate presence, with the incumbent management fully in charge. Ironically, top managers do not often speak of survival or cite it as a key strategic objective, perhaps because such talk might carry negative or defensive overtones, out of keeping with their confidence-inspiring leadership role. Yet their desire for organizational survival—and the professional survival allied with it—is implicit in everything they do. The preservation and enhancement of the firm's future are the essence of planning. Freedom from unfriendly acquisition or stockholder revolt and the continuity of existing top management are inextricably bound up with organizational survival in the broader sense.

Translated into practical terms, organizational survival means that management must always command sufficient corporate purchasing power to support the firm's vital functions. Therefore the firm's demand for funds must be balanced by the supply so that management will never be forced to default on expenditures essential to its competitive strategy. Assuring that this balance exists is the financial goal system's central purpose, as shall be seen hereafter.

Closely related to survival is a second motive which also has strong implications for financial planning: management's desire for independence: the freedom to make decisions and take action without consulting parties external to the enterprise. Such freedom is relative, of course, because no management can be completely independent of the outside world. But when given a choice, management will opt for more independence rather than less, whether it is dealing with government regulators, potential acquiring parents, or lenders negotiating contractual covenants. Even insiders such as shareholders and board members may become an object of concern in this regard, if they seem disposed to challenge management's real or assumed prerogatives.

Management's third motive, self-sufficiency, follows logically from this desire for independence. It derives, at least in part, from the managers' perception of the economic environment. Believing that their enterprise exists in a hostile, competitive world, they are reluctant to be dependent on other, equally self-interested external parties for their vital needs. Corporate managers talk a great deal about trust and loyalty, probably because they are precious and scarce resources in the rough-

and-tumble competitive world. In practice, they fall back on self-reliance and self-sufficiency as the best guarantors of survival.

Lastly, the managers' need for self-fulfillment or success influences the way in which they develop their corporate mission and manage their firm's resources. Given to likening themselves to professional athletes engaged in the competitive game of business, they look for specific visible measures of achievement, personally and organizationally. As the most objective criterion of performance, financial goals inevitably play a major role in fulfilling their expectations. In fact, these goals often take on a life of their own, quite apart from what they say about the ultimate success of the underlying business mission. They can even provide some consolation if the business fails and the game ends. To have scored against the opposition in the closing moments of play enables the individual manager to survive the pain of losing and come back to play again.

In seeking a rationale for management's strategic choices, this study does not go beyond these four basic motives. This is not to say that individual managers do not, at times, transcend organizational and personal self-interest to act in the interest of parties other than the career professionals who run the company. On the contrary, many corporate managers are truly convinced of their responsibilities to their external constituencies, particularly their shareholders. And to this extent they do look beyond the organization itself in their goals and motives. However, our observations also suggest that when push comes to shove, the organizational and personal motives cited above prove to be the most reliable predictors of management's behavior.

Maximizing Corporate Wealth

These motives are generally consistent with the financial objective that guided the top managers of the companies studied: the maximization of corporate wealth. Corporate wealth is *that wealth over which management has effective control* and which is an assured source of funds, at least within the limits of meaningful strategic planning. In practical terms it is cash, credit, and other corporate purchasing power by which management commands goods and services. Thus it is wealth vital to the organization's survival, wealth which the enterprise cannot or will not do without, because it is essential to its business mission. In this way corporate wealth differs considerably from the shareholder value which is central to much financial theory.

Stock market values are prospective, uncertain, and determined in great part by parties external to the business organization itself. The public equity market estimates these values by calculating and recalculating the present value of the future stream of benefits to be derived from a share of ownership. Presumably, these estimates are related to the management's ability to add to its store of economic wealth. Yet market values remain intangible until and unless the shareholders decide to exercise their claims on the company by selling their stock. In this sense their wealth becomes real only when it has been separated from the company; it is wealth management must do without.

In contrast, corporate wealth is immediate, certain, and meaningfully affected by those within the organization. By enhancing that wealth—and increasing the purchasing power at its disposal—management cannot fail to enhance its firm's competitive well-being and survival. Capital is a major competitive weapon. Access to a generous supply of funds can assure the business a dominant market position. Money can buy crucial time in which to act or await an improved environment. All other things being equal, therefore, the greater the store of corporate wealth, the less likely the chance of failure and the greater management's comfort level.

Similarly, an increase in corporate wealth has a beneficial effect upon the organization of which management is a part. Vigorous and sustained corporate expansion can attract and hold superior managerial and supervisory talent, as well as benefit individual corporate leaders. Upward mobility, breadth of experience, influence, financial and psychic rewards—all are more widely available in a growing corporation. Consequently, there are compelling organizational reasons to maximize corporate wealth in addition to the competitive reasons cited above.

Simultaneously, however, the wish to be independent and self-sufficient tempers management's drive for maximum corporate growth by restricting the pool of available capital. For example, a management may decide to forgo certain external sources of funds because they threaten to involve outsiders in resource-allocation decisions. Or it may fear to accept funds that seem likely to be withdrawn at a critical point in the firm's strategic development. Thus corporate managers trade off maximum economic scale for greater control of their resources and/or greater assurance that those resources will be loyal (i.e., that they will represent an enduring commitment to the corporation). These issues are central to management's strategic use of debt financing and they may apply to equity sources as well.

Considerations such as these remind us that corporate wealth is a more complex phenomenon than may at first appear. The form purchasing power takes, the certainty of its availability, and the timing of its accessibility are all as important as the total dollars involved, if not more so. For example, some purchasing power will be completely fungible, while other forms will be tied to specific use. Similarly, the certainty of availability will differ, even among resources over which management feels it has effective control. Vying with one another for internal funds, managers may engage in negotiations just as uncertain—and as delicate—as those undertaken with external investors. Finally, funds can come too late—or too soon—to support critical strategic investment.

Interestingly, the literal interpretation of discounted cash flow—that sooner is always better—does not always apply in practice. Instead, top managers must pace the inflow of funds, as well as their outflow, so that the timing of critical needs coincides with the availability of critical sources. Otherwise they run the risk that funds will arrive too soon and be unavailable by the time they are needed, because of misallocations. Managers must develop their financial plans with an eye for both the amount of their corporate purchasing power and its rate of flow. Sufficient stocks of cash and credit must be accumulated to support the enterprise's competitive activities, current and immediately prospective. Defaults on expenditures critical to the integrity of the firm's competitive strategy must not occur because the demand for funds has been allowed to outpace the supply.

The recognition that corporate wealth is multifaceted and that a maximization process necessarily involves tradeoffs to achieve the advantage desired suggests that the now familiar debate over satisficing versus maximization may be moot in the day-to-day flow of resource-related decisions.[3] The importance of wealth to a corporation or an individual is always relative to perceived needs. The higher the ratio of available resources to defined needs, the less compelling the concern for absolute dollars and the greater the opportunity to enhance other dimensions of wealth or respond to other priorities. Thus, on occasion, management's desired end may dictate less wealth for a time rather than more because corporate wealth is only one of several means to attain the end. For example, in building a dominant market position, management may choose to underprice the product to buy market share in preference to creating a financial war chest for vigorous competitive response.

Multiple Constituencies, Multiple Goals

Although organizational self-interest is management's central focus as it seeks to create and maximize corporate wealth, the enterprise and its managers do not exist in a vacuum. On the contrary, corporate managers must secure the continuing cooperation of a number of key interest groups or constituencies to achieve their objectives. Consequently they must weigh the effects of their decisions on a variety of partners as they develop their corporate goals and strategy.[4]

Typically statements of corporate purpose, such as the one cited at the beginning of this chapter, refer to four corporate partners or constituencies. These are the capital market of lenders and shareholders; the product market, which includes suppliers and host communities as well as customers; the organization itself, with particular emphasis on the managerial, technical, and supervisory personnel who are the key career employees; and society or the public at large. However, the last of these differs significantly from the others in two important respects. First, society has no clearcut role to play in the firm's ongoing operations. Second, little hard evidence exists to demonstrate the impact of a heightened corporate social conscience on management's goals or resource allocations.

This is not to say that all corporate references to society's well-being are fluff or window dressing. Managers believe that their products and services provide real value added for the consumer. Most, if not all, earnestly want to believe that the work they and their corporations are doing is central to the national interest and that "each of the communities [in which we operate] is better for our presence," as one company observed. Managements also vary greatly in responding to public pressure for improvements in the physical, economic, and human environments in which they operate, particularly when substantial funding is involved. Although some see their proper responsibility in terms of the minimum required by law, others take a leadership role.

However, these managements also tended to take a narrow, fundamentally economic view of their primary social responsibility by defining it as the provision of goods and services at a price which assures a return to the investor and funds the firm's continuity. In addition, it was clear that society's primary leverage on the corporation (apart from direct legal enforcement) was exerted through the forces of the product market: the power of consumers, employees, and host communities to protect their self-interest through the discipline of active negotiation and competition in the market place. For all these reasons, this study excludes society from its analysis of management's multiple constituencies and goals.

Among the other three groups, the capital market has traditionally stood first and foremost. Indeed, this study departs from standard financial theory in arguing that several constituencies are legitimately recognized in management's goals. Socially and legally, capitalism has tended to look only at a firm's owners in assigning benefits and assessing management's responsibilities. Consequently, most analyses are predicated on the assumption that the pursuit of any specific business mission—and the creation of corporate wealth to support it—simply extends management's duty to create wealth for the owners.[5] Thus they focus on the benefits returned to an investor/owner by a high return on investment rather than on the accumulation of corporate wealth. Dividends, capital gains, and growth in earning per share take precedence over growth in retained earnings and sales.

However, we need to recognize that in practice the capital market is not as monolithic as these analyses assume. For one thing, the capital market includes lenders whose interests center on questions of risk and credit worthiness. For another, the shareholders themselves are a diverse group with interests that often diverge. Some focus on dividends; others on capital gains. Some are in the market for a week or two; some for years on end. Some are loyal to management; others are hostile. Managers often consider themselves typical shareholders.[6] Yet professional investment analysts would be unlikely to agree that the portrait management draws accurately captures the characteristics of the investors they serve. Largely if not entirely undiversified, heavily dependent on this particular enterprise to realize his or her investment objectives, fiercely loyal, entirely satisfied with existing management, highly optimistic about the company's future: this is a loyal shareholder cut to management's cloth. But reality is often more complex, as the analyst rightly perceives.

Legal and philosophical considerations aside, the capital market's primary power lies in its capacity to deny management access to critical resources at a time when the firm's short-term or long-term survival is at stake. Management's responsiveness to investor priorities is therefore likely to be directly proportional to the degree and persistence of its dependence on external sources of funding. Predictably, the corporate officer most often assigned the task of responding to the shareholders is the chief financial officer whose responsibilities include fund raising and dividend policy.

The power of the product market constituency is derived from the fact that, collectively, it defines the economic environment within which the firm must achieve and sustain a viable income stream. Composed of customers, suppliers, union members, government agencies, and host communities, this is a diverse group and one whose interests are often in conflict. At times those interests can be negotiated unilaterally because they are specific to a particular coalition (e.g., a union). But, for the most part, the product market's primary disciplinary power is imposed by the firm's competitors rather than the constituents themselves. This is so because management cannot sustain strong and substantial product-market positions unless it can match or better its competitors in meeting its constituents' needs. Supplies must be continuous and dependable. Prices must be competitive and quality satisfactory. Production must be state of the art.

Considerations such as these powerfully influence corporate investment and funding profiles. They also help to explain why a firm's strategy will inevitably be dominated by a particular product market (with its unique industry characteristics) at any given stage in its history. As has been noted, real asset investment is not frictionless. Management must sustain some given level of financial and human investment as a condition of playing its particular business game. As long as these effective barriers to exit exist, therefore, the firm will be the captive of its particular product-market constituency and management must take account of its requirements.

The importance of product-market priorities in shaping corporate goals can be seen in the extent to which these goals track and measure product-market performance through comparison with specific competitors. Success in the capital market, as measured by a superior bond rating, price-earnings ratio, or effective yield on the latest term loan, is an appropriate cause for rejoicing. But it is likely to have to compete for attention, particularly among the managerial rank and file, with success in the product market as it is measured in global coverage, productive capacity, industry rank, and that ultimate of competitive excellence, share of market.

The real purpose of these goals and their intended beneficiaries may at times disappear from managements' consciousness amid the pressure and complexity of daily events. Inevitably, means and ends become entangled in the process of getting things done. But product-market goals retain their individual importance nonetheless, particularly for product-line managers, who are the people most responsible for year-to-year sales and profit performance. To be successful these managers must be alert to the impact of top management's decisions and action on the product market constituency and must represent their interests to the top management group.

Management's third constituency is its own organization: the key career employees on whom it relies for the success of its strategic plans. Valued for their unique abilities (real or perceived), these people are an important factor in management's decision-making process. Top management considers them a scarce resource and it seeks to develop and sustain their loyalty through its corporate objectives. For example, managers will often speak about their company's growth in terms of their need to attract and hold talented individuals.

Because top managers are themselves a part of the organization, they tend to feel a strong sense of identity with their company's career employees. Yet it would be a mistake to assume that they are thinking only of their own self-interest when they speak about organizational priorities. Their leadership role carries with it requirements different in degree and kind from those that belong to the rank and file. It also affords their personal needs and preferences a wider play. Ultimately, therefore, top management is called upon to represent both the organization and itself, in addition to arbitrating and balancing the entire range of constituent priorities essential to cooperative effort.

As with the other constituencies, the organization's power to influence corporate goals lies in its capacity to have an identifiable and substantial impact on the firm's success. (Part of a manager's organizational identity depends on his or her belief in the uniqueness and importance of the organization's ability and experience.) In addition, it is furthered by management's tendency to believe that its career employees are uniquely talented and able by virtue of their experience with the company. Whether this is so may be open to question, just as the importance and uniqueness of the company's goods and services may be questioned by a dispassionate equity investor or customer. But the organization cannot be so objective, and conditions that develop, stimulate, and sustain the commitment of talented individuals are central to management's financial goals.

Financial Goals and the Corporate Mission

Corporate financial goals statements provide an objective context in which management's multiple constituencies are brought together. There the interests of each must be reflected in one or more of the quantitative criteria that direct the flow of corporate funds. These criteria (target growth and return figures, projected dividends, debt ratios, and the like) are rough but powerful representations of more complex issues. In effect they stand as constant reminders of the complex environment which must be permissive, if not actively benevolent, if management's corporate mission is to be accomplished.

Not all corporate managers recognize the need for formal statements. Even among the companies studied a small minority chose to leave their financial and corporate goals unarticulated. However, their companies shared certain special characteristics that do much to explain this choice. Unlike the majority of large corporations, they tended to be engaged in a narrow and uniform set of business activities, to have experienced a relatively stable industrial environment for an extended period of time, and to have enjoyed a degree of success financially. In addition, the managers had a widely shared and clearly understood sense of what was expected of them. Thus they felt able to forgo the creation of formal financial goals statements.

Most large corporations do not conform to this pattern. On the contrary, they tend to have experienced one or more of the following conditions at some stage in their history: business activities have been diversified; decentralized management has become necessary; the environment has changed significantly; the top management team has been unstable; obvious success has not been attained. The need for formal financial goals can become evident under any of these circumstances, particularly if formal planning is also becoming increasingly popular. Moreover, the assertion of these goals can become a vehicle for uniting the organization behind a coordinated strategy for improvement.

In using the term financial goals this study refers to *the subset of corporate goals concerned with the business entity's financial condition and performance and with management's related actions and decisions involving the acquisition, custody, and disposition of corporate funds.* However, as previous comments indicate, the range of objectives served by these goals is broad. Some are clearly financially oriented. For example, management will use its goals to set performance targets and deadlines, to measure and reward accomplishments, to guide and set boundaries on middle managers' choices, and to set standards for the acquisition and allocation of financial resources. But financial goals also contribute to objectives less obviously related to the flow of funds within the firm. Among the companies studied, for example, corporate financial goals were employed to establish a sense of corporate identity, uniqueness, and legitimacy, to provide unity of purpose across a competitive organization and gain consensus, to assert vigorous, ambitious leadership and stake out territorial prerogatives, within and without the firm, and to signal necessary changes of direction. In sum these goals were as important for what they said about management's strategy and objectives as for the particular performance indices they specified.

Financial goals speak in various ways as signals of management's direction and emphasis. Target percentages, absolute dollar figures, and comparative standards attest to the level at which management chooses to compete. Resource allocation and funding decisions reveal divisional strategies and corporate commitments. Tradeoffs among competing goals indicate which constituencies are favored at the moment or which seem to have the upper hand.

This last holds true because, as has been seen, particular financial goals can be correlated with the self-interest of one or another of management's corporate partners. In practice, of course, nothing prevents several constituencies from reaping the rewards of the same financial objective. For example, it is reasonable to assume that both a company's shareholders and its suppliers will benefit from greater corporate growth. And yet, growth achieved through diversification tends to weaken the influence of particular product-market constituencies. Likewise, a corporate growth objective unqualified by a definition of risk and rate-of-return targets may not serve the best interests of the shareholders. Thus, it is possible to define conditions under which corporate growth would be seen as desirable only by those whose careers and fortunes were closely related to the company's survival, health, and economic importance.

Sharp tests of constituencies' priorities such as this usually occur only under extreme circumstances. However, each of the corporate partners will have a decided opinion about the relative importance of management's financial goals. Moreover, they or their representatives within the top management team will expect to see those opinions—and their own self-interest—recognized in the company's financial plans. Corporate financial goals statements provide an important and appropriate vehicle for management's response, as the one which follows indicates.

This brief, clear, and emphatic declaration of corporate direction was drawn up by top management as part of a concerted drive for higher levels of achievement. It is reproduced as it originally appeared, except that all specific references which could identify the company have been deleted. As the reader will see, the statement creates some very specific expectations for the company's managers.

CORPORATE MISSION

> To market [product lines] profitably (i.e., transcend in ROI, Earnings
> Growth, Market Leadership, Technical Innovation)

CORPORATE TARGETS

Qualitative

Provide long-term investors with a superior return on capital
Develop [product-market expertise]
Create a balanced portfolio of product lines
Manage [corporate] money astutely, conservatively
Make [corporate] identity with people real

Quantitative

Reach a 15% ROI (companywide)
Grow in volume and profitability
    Sales growth 50% greater than GNP, inflation adjusted
    Profit growth 30% greater than sales growth, inflation adjusted
Other financial targets
    Debt ratio less than 25% of total capital
    Bond Rating: AA
    Dividend Payout: 33% of total earnings
Market leadership: Be Number One in market segment

CORPORATE STRATEGIES

General

Don't lose our place
Build from there

Specific

Beat inflation
Manage the cycles
Improve present businesses
Be a world leader
Support innovation

Each of management's constituencies could recognize its own interests in particular parts of this statement. Shareholders would appreciate a "superior return on capital," profit growth in excess of inflation-adjusted sales growth, and a defined dividend payout. Lenders could identify with a specific, conservative debt limit and AA bond rating. Customers would respond favorably to management's commitment to sustained leadership in particular product lines and to the customer satisfaction which that market and technological leadership implies. Career employees would be stimulated by the potential for upward mobility in a company which plans to outgrow GNP by 50 percent, inflation adjusted.

Top managers, too, could take satisfaction in these corporate goals. Their high-performance orientation meshes with the personal drives and organizational motives that underlie the business mission. They are also designed to assure the active cooperation of all constituencies essential to the firm's success in its business mission. What cannot yet be known is whether these goals are compatible with one another. Could management achieve all its goals simultaneously, or would it have to assign priorities and make tradeoffs among them? To answer questions such as these we must look beyond individual goals and constituencies to the flow of funds within the firm.

The Management of the Flow of Funds

Tradeoffs among competing financial goals take on real and specific meaning in decisions that affect the flow of funds. An investment proposal promoted by the historically dominant division of a major corporation illustrates how these tradeoffs occur. A new technology, developed abroad but available under license, opened up the possibility of a huge new market for the company's basic raw materials. The price was high. It required a major reconversion of some of the company's productive capacity and an investment of hundreds of millions of dollars. All aspects of the proposal were studied exhaustively and at length, including the prospective return on investment. The latter study revealed that the most likely ROI, on a discounted cash flow basis, was less than 5 percent.

A long and vigorous debate ensued between divisional and corporate management. The division, true to its product-market orientation, pressed the potential for growth and the urgency of beating the competition. They hoped to seize a substantial share of the new market, perhaps even execute a preemptive strike. By contrast, the managers at corporate headquarters were deeply disturbed by the apparent absence of near-term returns consistent with the major risks involved. They knew that they would have to obtain some of the necessary funds from the capital market and that they would have to account for the return on that investment capital.

In the end, the issue was resolved by the approval of a $50 million investment in a pilot plant conversion designed to buy better information and more time to clarify the major uncertainties. The decision was clearly a modest response to the organizational constituency—a signal to the division that despite the poor ROI prospects, its commitment to the company's growth was recognized and valued, and that it would live to fight another day. However, the tension this decision created was reflected by the chief executive when he commented several years later: "I will go to my grave wondering if I made the right decision." As a man who had risen to the top by the financial route, he was keenly aware of the capital market's priorities. But as a chief executive he knew that the company had to survive in its traditional product markets, with opportunities as they were, and against aggressive competitors who might look at the same evidence and reach different conclusions. To accomplish this corporate mission he had to have the active cooperation and support of the people who were sponsoring this initiative. Thus the necessary tradeoffs came about not as a matter of course, from some predetermined ranking of constituent interests, but rather from the perceived benefit to organizational survival, independence, and managerial accomplishment.

Notes

1. Donaldson and Lorsch, *Decision Making at the Top*, pp. 79–109.

2. *Ibid.*

3. See, for example, Robert N. Anthony, "The Trouble with Profit Maximization," *Harvard Business Review* 38 (November-December 1960): 126–34.

4. The concept of corporate partners is a well-established one. See, for example, Richard M. Cyert and James G. March, *A Behavioral Theory of the Firm* (Englewood Cliffs, NJ: Prentice-Hall, 1963), pp. 26–43.

5. See, for example, Eugene V. Rostow, "To Whom and For What Ends Are Corporate Managements Responsible?" in *The Corporation in Modern Society*, ed. Edward S. Mason (Cambridge, MA: Harvard University Press, 1959), pp. 46–71.

6. In the past much has been made of the identity of the management and shareholder viewpoints because of stock option plans and top management's substantial stock holdings. (Even though stock option plans have diminished in

importance in recent years, it is clear that most top managers are also share-holders whose equity is a significant portion of their personal wealth.) However, the fact that managers are typically *undiversified* shareholders whose equity wealth is totally dependent on the success of their enterprise and therefore indis-tinguishable in origin from their compensation as managers has often been over-looked. The shareholder/manager is the epitome of the loyal shareholder, and he (or she) tends to view the ideal shareholder as having the same loyalty (or dependence) that he has himself.

3

The Network of Individual Financial Goals

Established Product Markets and Strategic Investment

At any given time, most industrial firms (including many of the largest) depend on a small number of distinct product-market positions for their primary income stream. Typically, these positions have been developed over years or decades of continuous activity and they are neither easily nor rapidly liquidated, even should management wish to do so. Considerable uncertainty surrounds major investment and disinvestment options, while economic, organizational, and psychological factors all argue against an exit decision. Meaningful opportunities to alter course occur infrequently, and they are often beyond management's ability to initiate.

Once management has made a serious commitment to a major product market, therefore, it tends to be locked into that particular environment. Each product market initiated requires a highly integrated set of investments. These investment requirements must be continuously funded if the firm is to maintain a credible competitive position in its chosen markets. Competitors, customers, suppliers, and employees all will judge management's serious intent by its ability and willingness to continue to place the firm's capital at risk. Should this capacity for continuous funding be called into question, the complex network of relationships supporting the firm's position quickly begins to unravel.

As a consequence of these competitive facts of life, few of management's funds are likely to be available for discretionary or *opportunistic* expenditures at any given time.[1] Instead, most are allocated to the strategic investments that support those product-market positions that are the firm's lifeblood. As one executive noted in describing his own company's financial plans, "something like ninety percent of the budget" could not be modified "without changing [management's] strategy." In a sense, these investments in existing product markets are comparable to the so-called "entitlement" portions of the federal budget which can neither be ignored nor modified in the short term.

The financial commitments required to sustain a competitive presence in a given product market reduce management's strategic investment choices to three elements: the selection of the particular product market in which to compete; the choice of the time to enter or withdraw; the choice of the *level* at which to compete (in terms of scale or share of market). Yet even this list effectively overstates the options most often presented to the management of mature enterprises whose primary income stream is derived from a number of established product-market positions. For these managers the prospect of withdrawing or harvesting is hedged about with important economic and psychological constraints. As one executive commented:

> We do a lot of talking about "harvesting" [mature product markets] but it gripes us to see a competitor take market share away. This business is "war games." We don't mind losing the occasional battle but we have to win the war. I don't really want to lose a battle, for example, to [name of a competitor]. They are testing us, judging our response time. We are not going to roll over. We are all highly competitive guys. As a result, we probably don't do as much harvesting as we should. It's hard for a manager to let go. There is no glory in harvesting.

Thus, the option of withdrawing from an established product market may be presented only rarely—even when clear indications of deteriorating returns exist.

The Compulsion to Grow

The drive to win, evident in the comment quoted above, is closely linked to management's desire for corporate growth. Top managers may ask, as one did, "Does [our company] need to grow?" But among the managements studied that question was rhetorical and the answer was always yes. Every company in the research sample adopted an open-ended growth objective; none aspired to be smaller, to grow to some specified level and stop, or to become fragmented. As one senior divisional president noted in an address to an in-house management conference, "I hope that none of us will question 'whether' and 'why' we must grow, and that we may discuss how, where, and when we must grow, with full confidence that growth is necessary—desirable and indeed inevitable for [our company]."

Evidence of this deep, almost instinctive, need for organizational growth can be found in the objective record of corporate financial goals (see Table 3-1). Almost every management used an explicit, companywide compound growth rate as a central element of its long-range planning. These corporate growth targets ranged from 8 percent to 17 percent, with a mean of 13 percent. In other words, on the average, management hoped to double its absolute sales dollars every five years. These goals were clearly chosen to challenge and stimulate the organization's growth, not to restrain it.

The management at Commodity Products II (one of two exceptions to this practice) also chose goals designed to ensure that the firm's reach would exceed its grasp. However, these managers saw no need to set a corporate growth target because theirs was a single-industry company with no current diversification plans. Consequently, they believed that growth objectives centered on preserving and improving share of market and industry rank provided adequate stimuli for corporate and divisional managers. These goals had a precise *relative* definition, and they did not need to be translated into absolute dollar figures or a growth rate independent of industry rank. (Indeed, such translation would effectively imply a reassessment of corporate strategy should the goal not be met by some predetermined date; but reassessment was not an option so far as current management was concerned.)

The link between corporate growth and the firm's existing product markets is found in goals relating to rank in industry and share of market. Usually these appear at the divisional level because specific targets vary from market to market. As Table 3-1 indicates, every company in the research sample, save one, had an explicit and aggressive share-of-market philosophy. Divisional managers were urged to increase their existing market share or defend their dominant position. Corporate managers strove to be Number One in every product market. Even the management at Technical Products I, the single exception, was very much aware of its competitive position within its industry.

Table 3-1. Sample Data on Growth Targets and Performance

Company		Share of Market Goal	Company Growth Rate		Industry Growth Rates		
			Target (%) (1978)	Average Actual Performance (%) (1968–1978)	Industry Average (%) (1968–1978)	Selected Competitors Mean (%)	Range (%)
Technical Products	I	Not an Objective	NA	20.0	NA	14.4	9–19
	II	Number One in Each Product Market	15	9.8	9.7	11.8	10.2–15.8
	III	Dominant Market Share	8	11.0	9.3	11.0	7.6–15.3
Consumer Products	I	Strong Focus on Rank in Industry	17	18.0	20.0	NA	NA
	II	SOM Target, by Product Market	12	15.5	9.3	13.0	11.7–14.7
	III	SOM Target, by Product Market	15	15.1	10.8	12.3	9.5–16.8
	IV	SOM Target, by Division	14	11.9	10.2	13.0	6.6–20.8
Commodity Products	I	Strong Emphasis on SOM, Market Leadership	15	11.5	8.8	10.0	8.5–12.7
	II	Increasing SOM, Focus on Rank in Industry	NA	11.5	NA	NA	NA
	III	SOM Target, by Product Market	10	9.3	10.2	10.8	9.8–12.0
Conglomerate	I	Divisional Goals: Increased SOM	8	7.5	9.0	11.6	6.6–18.1
	II	Increasing SOM	10	7.2	9.0	11.6	6.6–18.1

Note. Because of product line diversity, the appropriate industry reference group is not always obvious. The tables in this volume follow management's lead by using the group of competitors the company tracked for its comparisons whenever possible. Nevertheless, considerable judgment had to be exercised in the selection process, so that only broad and tentative conclusions are justified. In addition, the size of the sample (when broken down into general classes) will not allow meaningful conclusions to be drawn about the two conglomerates. Differences in the method of calculating ratios have been eliminated by converting all targets and results to a common basis.

More than management's own competitiveness is required to explain these choices. Aggressive sales goals also reflect the belief that market share is the cornerstone of profitability. This widespread belief is the most powerful and pervasive force behind management's impulse to sustain new investment in established product markets. As one executive observed, while describing his company's investment strategy:

> We want to be in a strong position everywhere. We say, "Do what you have to do to retain a leadership position, even in the short run." Of course, over the long run, you can only stay a leader if you have the best cost position, so we must pay attention to that. But get the strongest leadership position and *that* is what is going to pay off.

Typically, these businessmen felt little need for objective proof that a rising market share would produce rising profit margins or that discontinuities in price/cost relationships would create new levels of profitability. Instead, these were taken as givens, as was their corollary—the assumption that a near-term improvement in the rate of return on investment was most readily brought about by additional investment in established markets. Again, one of the managers articulated these assumptions when he said,

> The variable I watch closely is penetration. We also watch ROI and contribution margin. If you go too far in penetration, your price structure goes to hell and you lose money. But, if we know that we have good costs and are a strong seller [i.e., little or no price discounting], it is axiomatic that with good market share we'll have the best profits.

Well-founded economic principles support management's conviction that industry leadership provides the greatest profit potential. Economies of scale, purchasing power, price leadership, access to resources, and barriers to entry are all relevant concepts, even though their power in individual markets must be carefully analyzed.[2] In addition, managers believe that industry leadership reduces uncertainty and increases competitive advantage because the company becomes the agent of change rather than its object. Working on the theory that the best defense is a good offense, top managers prefer initiating changes themselves to responding to their competitors' initiatives. However, the drive for market leadership also means that management's particular product-market strategy and its level of investment will be driven by the growth rate of the industry itself. Consequently, corporate growth objectives must equal or exceed anticipated industry growth for competitive strategy to be judged successful.

As the data in Table 3-1 suggest, these corporate managers were inclined to view the industry growth rate as a floor rather than a ceiling. They also applied a similar perspective to their own performance record. Of the ten companies with an explicit growth rate objective, seven equaled or exceeded the historical average industry growth rate, while two of the remaining three equaled or exceeded their own ten-year historical average growth rate. Only one company in the sample had a current growth rate objective which fell short of both the industry and the company average. In seeking an explanation for this exception, it is useful to remember that most companies experience alternating periods of growth and consolidation. Therefore, the dominant mode in any particular year (as indicated by management's target) may not accord with the company's long-term direction. In the case of Technical Products III, the company at issue here, 1978 was a year of consolidation. The company had been shaken by a serious financial crisis in 1974–75, and management was clearly focused on restraining new investment and improving the balance sheet.

Although the company's target growth rates are initially determined by its existing product-market environment, other considerations also come into play as corporate goals are set. Among them are management's assumptions about the benefits growth provides for its organizational and capital-market constituencies. In organizational terms these assumptions are justified. Above-average growth does increase the opportunity for upward mobility, and it therefore helps to "attract and hold high caliber people," as one company noted in its statement of corporate purpose. But it is less apparent that growth benefits the capital market, as management also often assumes.

The advantage of growth for the company's lenders lies in the added security it supplies. An increase in assets and earning power funded by retained earnings shifts the risk-return tradeoff in their favor. However, the presumed advantage for the shareholder is open to question. Given that chief executives tend to identify most readily with loyal and undiversified shareholders like themselves, it is not surprising that they endow the latter with their own perspective on growth. Nevertheless, an objective, independent investor could reasonably be expected to question the assumptions behind an open-ended commitment to growth, particularly if they seemed to be leading to inappropriate investment decisions. Free to diversify and to invest in the competition, he or she is primarily interested in maximizing rates of return per unit of invested capital, for any given risk level, over an entire securities portfolio. Hence, the independent investor need not share management's preeminent concern for this particular company's growth and vitality.

Management's open-ended pursuit of growth also reflects its commitment to increasing the firm's invested capital through the expansion of productive assets and expenditures for product research, development, and marketing. The relationships between these investment expenditures and growth in the volume of operations are complex and varied in practice because the former depend on many circumstantial factors. Past cycles of expenditure, existing slack in the system, technological change, anticipated growth, the lumpiness of increments of capacity, relative rates of inflation past, present, and future—all affect the level of operating and capital expenditures during any given planning period. However, for general planning purposes, corporate managers normally assume that the ratio of investment in assets to sales volume will remain relatively stable over the customary five-year planning horizon.[3] Thus their sales goals necessarily have a direct impact on the absolute scale of the assets they control as Table 3-2, prepared by one of the companies in the research sample, indicates.

Moreover, size per se appears to have been important to top managers for organizational and personal reasons as well as for competitive ones, even though no one identified his or her objectives in these terms. Increasing sophistication in the planning process tends to disguise this thrust, as rates of growth sound more modest than the absolute dollar goals they have replaced. But such reformulations reflect management's greater awareness of the ongoing process of capital formation rather than

Table 3-2. Comparison of Rates of Growth in Sales and Assets

Industry Group	Annual Rate of Growth (1966–1975)	
	Sales (%)	Assets (%)
Standard & Poor's 400 Industrials	11.0	10.2
Seven Drug Companies	13.5	15.1
Seven Cosmetic Companies	13.3	15.8
Ten Packaged Food Companies	12.3	12.4
Six Soap Companies	12.6	11.3
Our own experience	14.8	14.7

a lack of interest in growth and volume. To say that you wish to be a billion dollar company by a specific date emphasizes the arrival. To say that you wish to grow at X percent per annum emphasizes the journey. Both statements can lead to the same destination.

Providing Appropriate Funds for Growth

Top management's commitment to continuous growth means that it must have a matching strategy for providing the requisite funds. Nowhere is this necessity more apparent than in the funding of existing product markets. There, as we have seen, market opportunities strongly influence the level of investment. Because of the high priority placed on productivity and increasing market share, this flow of funds is commonly perceived as mandated, at least in the near term, by the firm's competitive environment. The basic competitive signal, both inside and outside the organization, relates to the perceived intensity of management's commitment to stay the course.

Within the competitive context the nature and degree of management's investment choices are functions of the planning horizon. This future period (generally lasting several years) is defined by management's contractual commitments to the organization and by the strategic commitments it imposes upon itself. As a rule, management will honor these commitments barring some major, unexpected shift in the economic environment. Thus it is unlikely that agreed-upon levels of financial support for given product markets will be changed significantly during the planning period. Essential investments in working capital and productive capacity will be defined by the volume of business management anticipates and the sources of these funds must match the company's perceived needs. Ironically, therefore, these funding needs tend to assume a degree of certainty beyond that justified by the facts. This occurs because the sales forecasts become the objectives which establish the basis for management's funding commitments to those charged with achieving them.

As management considers the flow of funds for strategic investments in established product markets, these assumptions tend to limit its options. As we shall see, corporate managers prefer sources that most nearly satisfy certain conditions. These include: availability on an open-ended and continuous basis; compatibility with the level of management's perceived needs; a high degree of certainty as to amount and timing; reasonable cost to the organization; and the absence of terms which would contravene management's normal prerogatives over its funds. Not all sources of funds satisfy these conditions.

The Limitations of the Public Capital Market

Top managers of major industrial corporations have had decades of individual experience with the capital market. Such experience tends to persuade many (probably most) that the public capital market is an untrustworthy ally when it comes to their corporation's vital interests. They recognize that the U.S. economy provides a well-organized and relatively efficient system for distributing private and institutional savings among various investing enterprises and that, by and large, the market is more than adequate to meet the needs of any individual business. But they also know that their enterprise does not survive by and large. It survives from moment to never-ending moment, or it does not survive at all.

Watching the public equity and debt markets' sharp cyclical fluctuations, therefore, many corporate managers come to believe in the reality of a market window for financing. This window opens and shuts at times not of their choosing, and its timing may or may not coincide with the vital needs of a particular competitive venture. Consequently, they are loathe to entrust the success of those ventures to the public markets, no matter how large and well-established the companies they direct.

It may come as a shock to hear a senior executive of a blue-chip, triple A corporation speak emotionally about the "threat to corporate survival" presented by the world economic and financial crises of 1974. But his company's radical restructuring of its investment and financial policy corroborates the sincerity of his remarks. The popular notion of an old-boy network with a collective interest in maintaining the status quo is quickly belied by the overriding self-interest which comes to the surface when a financial crisis occurs.

The objective evidence of the external capital markets' limited role in funding established product markets lies in the collective experience of the mature industrial companies studied. In this combined record of financing, covering more than 120 company-years, there were only two issues of common or preferred stock for cash. These accounted for about one percent of the $8.5 billion of new long-term capital added to the companies during this period. (By coincidence an equal amount of equity was repurchased so that the net addition was zero.[4])

The managements which made use of the public equity market as a contingency reserve did so under extraordinary circumstances and outside their normal funding frameworks. These companies did not *plan* to use public equity for cash. In one case the company's domestic market was growing at a compound rate approaching 30 percent a year, while its foreign market was increasing by 40 percent at the same time. Thus the company could not keep up with the market without outside assistance, despite strong profits. However, management was reluctant to repeat the experience and made it a point to "try to run the company so that equity is not the only alternative." As one of the executives observed,

> At the time we sold equity, we were driven to it by the growth rate—the necessity to survive. We were caught in a competitive squeeze and we had to break out. You do what you have to do. Now we are more reluctant to sell equity. We are more concerned with shareholder attitudes. We didn't ask them.

In the other case management could no longer defer a major upgrading of its productive capacity, even though years of depressed industry conditions had weakened the company's financial position so that cooperation from its lenders could only be obtained by selling new equity. Beforehand, the top managers feared the worst. As one of them remembered:

> We were prepared to go down to 20 percent below book and we prepared the case as low as $X. [And] there remains a question in my mind: How low were we really willing to go? We had to sell the stock [if we were going to protect market share].

In the event the issue went better than had been expected. The stock sold just under book value, and management declined a competing investment banker's proposal to sell more. Nevertheless, the extremity of the situation is obvious.

Students of corporate finance have often wondered why industrial managements do not use new external equity more extensively to fund the normal growth of established businesses. No single answer suffices because the issues are complex and involve subjective as well as objective factors. However, this study calls attention to two considerations that influence management's decisions. The first is corporate leaders' inevitable disposition to regard their equity as undervalued—good times or bad. This disposition results from their plans and commitment to better performance in the future and from their conviction that outsiders are always ill-informed. Expectations for next year's sales and earnings always look better to the insiders who have responsibility—and the self-confidence—for delivering them than last year's results do to a skeptical and detached investor. Thus, *next year* always promises a better price.

A second deterrent to the use of equity in funding ongoing investment is management's preference for continuous, reliable, and predictable sources of funds. In a mature organization the necessity to turn to the public equity market for supplemental funds is often seen as a public admission of misjudgment or mismanagement. Had management accurately foreseen its capital requirements (for the established product markets), it would have priced its products more aggressively, controlled expenses more carefully, or retained more earnings (i.e., it would have conserved cash in such a way as to fund the growth on its own). Thus, these managers attached a negative connotation to the market signal associated with a new equity issue. Management abhors surprises, especially those that are considered bad news.

Use of the public debt market is another matter. In this regard management was prepared to fund some of its ongoing strategic needs from a source which can be unreliable at times. Of the $8.5 billion of new funds invested by these companies between 1969 and 1978, long-term debt funded some 26 percent. The strategy for dealing with the attendant uncertainty can be summed up in one word: conservatism. In essence, the managers of these mature industrial companies sought to conduct their own affairs so that *they* could *always* borrow if necessary, even in bad times. They did so by keeping their borrowing within tight limits and by providing wide margins of safety over and above the lender's minimum lending rules. They made it a practice to live within the standards of an A credit rating at the least and within moderate debt/equity ratios. As a result, they were in a position to regard debt as an automatic extension of internally generated funds and to treat it, for planning purposes at least, as though it were an assured, off-balance sheet, liquid asset reserve. Each increment of retained earnings could be assumed to bring an additional unit of debt capacity along with it.

These practices and attitudes indicate that top management views the capital market as essentially *private* insofar as its firm's vital requirements are concerned. These corporate managers expect that the equity required to sustain their established businesses will be generated from within, and that any necessary debt will be readily forthcoming from a captive public debt equity market. The evidence of their thinking is apparent in the companies' investment statistics. During the period under review, 74 percent of the new funds were generated internally, with the balance provided by long-term debt with an overall debt/equity ratio of 1 to 3.

A Strategy of Self-Sufficiency

The financial strategy that emerges from a study of these industrial firms can best be characterized as one of self-sufficiency. It springs from management's desire for self-preservation in an environment generally regarded as hostile and unpredictable. In addition, it accords with a business climate in which intense competition is the norm and which lacks a public or private safety net for those who fall. Thus, financial self-sufficiency complements the organizational goals of survival and independence which are basic to management's corporate mission.

In practice, this strategy means that managements rely heavily on retained earnings to meet the demand for funds from their existing businesses. Retained earnings are particularly appropriate for this purpose because they are the source about which management has the best information and over which it has the greatest control. Accordingly, they lend themselves to the close coordination in the flow of funds which strategic investments require. As has been seen, corporate managers work with most of their strategic investment budget tightly set; they cannot separate the demand for funds from their supply. As one senior financial executive observed, "One can't pull back from long-term goals simply because of short-term changes."

That the managers themselves thought about their financial strategies in terms of self-sufficiency was clear from their comments and planning documents. A colleague of the executive quoted above made just this point in a speech whose theme was repeated by his peers in other companies. Addressing the relationship between earnings retention and strategic investment, he observed:

> In theory, a business which can compound its investment worth at a higher rate than the investors' acceptable rate of return should be allowed to retain all its earnings. . . . In the real world, there are very

few companies which have achieved [this] performance level. . . . Typically, companies with good growth or internal compounding potential will pay out only a fairly low proportion of earnings. . . . The important fact is the [company] has a [disengaged] cash flow requirement of [$X] million a year. Therefore, it is evident that the company's present operations must run so that [$X] million will be pumped directly into the cash box. . . . For most of our businesses, the net asset investment requirement should be financed without increasing our desired debt/equity balance because a great many of our businesses are characterized by a "maintain" [vs. "build" or "harvest"] strategy. . . . A common thread which you have probably detected . . . is that each S.B.U. which is in the "maintain" area is expected to . . . finance its own cash requirements as well as pay for debt and dividend servicing. *These self-sustaining performance goals for most units are a necessity.* Hopefully, we should attempt to surpass a mere self-sustaining profit requirement and generate enough cash to finance fundamental new growth potentials. (Emphasis added.)

In the following chapter we shall look more closely at the ways in which the concept of financial self-sufficiency influences the character of management's financial goal setting. For now, we must turn to the price management pays for its independence and control over strategic investment. That price is *the need to live within limits.* The sources of funds that are continuous, predictable, reliable, and free of discretionary restrictions are also limited in magnitude and in timing. Management must order its strategic investments to fit the available capital at the available time; it must plan carefully and live within its plans. Further, each business unit or division must learn to accomplish its objectives with its share of plannable resources—or find some way to renegotiate allocations with its internal competitors.

As should be readily apparent, this price tag significantly diminishes the possibility of spontaneous or opportunistic investment. The internal capital market as it has been defined is a finite capital market. Unless management is willing to expose its strategies to the uncertainties of the external capital market and to the judgments of independent investors, it cannot escape this limitation. Most managements are reluctant to do so.

Nevertheless, the top managers of publicly traded industrial corporations do not ignore the capital market as they design their goals and strategies. On the contrary, philosophical bias and formal responsibility combine to focus their attention on the shareholders, the group which presumably controls the firm's underlying risk capital. It is this group's loyalty which must be strengthened along with its disposition to fund the enterprise in the future. Consequently, the shareholders occupy a prominent position as management thinks about its financial goals.

Dominant Supply-Related Financial Goals

Most corporate financial goals statements begin with a summary of the company's intentions on behalf of its shareholders, as in the following quote:

> [The Company's] primary criterion for growth is earnings per share on common equity. Its objective is to avoid a year-to-year decline in earnings per share and to achieve an average growth rate of [X%] or more per year in current dollar terms.
>
> [The Company] believes that its stockholders have a major interest in total return, i.e., dividends plus market appreciation. Growth and sustainability of dividends will be important considerations, and dividend payout will fall generally in the range of [X%] of reported earnings.
>
> Return on stockholders' equity would be expected to reach [Y%] in the early 1980s.
>
> [With respect to acquisitions] the overriding factor should be the long-term return to the stockholder. Therefore, any dilution of earnings per share must be offset by an anticipated improvement in the price/earnings ratio.
>
> [The Company] will strive to enhance the market value of its stock as measured by its price/earnings ratio compared to other manufacturing companies. This ratio is expected to be consistently better than the ratio of the Dow Jones Industrial Average by the early 1980s.

This is an impressive and unquestionably sincere statement; but certain qualifications must be noted. The first grows out of the fact that management determines neither the market value of its stock nor its price/earnings ratio. Consequently, it cannot manage these financial values in the same way in which it manages its corporate wealth (i.e., by allocating and utilizing the human and financial resources at its disposal). Management can strive to improve its market standing by its influence over the underlying variables it considers most important: earnings, dividends, return on equity, and the number of shares outstanding. But the belief that good management in these areas will translate sooner or later into an increase in shareholder wealth remains a leap of faith.

A second set of qualifications centers on the managers' beliefs about their shareholders' priorities. Although these beliefs are well intentioned, nothing guarantees that they are correct, nor that they will hold constant over time. Further, as we have seen, top managers tend to identify most readily with loyal shareholders like themselves, who understand clearly the company's circumstances and objectives, accept and support the existing strategy, have confidence in management, and are committed to long-term results and rewards. These shareholders are the antithesis of portfolio investors who trade in and out of the company's stock and make alternative investments easily. Loyal shareholders have a strong bias toward the reinvestment of earnings and they share the managers' conviction that "we can use the dollars better than the shareholder, and we assume he knows that when he buys the stock."

For these reasons, investor-oriented goals tend to be replaced by goals that define the rate of flow of immediate corporate purchasing power. The primary components of these dominant supply-related goals are: the target return on investment; the acceptable limits of dividend payout; and the limit in the debt/equity ratio. In other words, management's financial planning focuses on goals which discipline the acquisition and allocation of funds rather than on shareholder priorities per se. References to equity values, price/earnings ratios, and earnings per share are rarely found in planning documents. Market-related financial goals such as the growth rate of earnings, the return on equity, and even the growth rate of earnings per share tend to disappear. For example, only four of the twelve companies consistently targeted E.P.S. in their internal goal-setting, while six never formally recognized an E.P.S. goal during the period under review.

A decade or more ago, corporate earnings objectives were commonly expressed in absolute terms: management chose a dollar figure or it set a target rate of growth for the company's absolute earnings. As financial planning became more refined, however, it became clear that the quantity of corporate earnings had to be related to their quality, lest absolute growth be purchased at the price of declining rates of return. Consequently, most managements have now switched to a target return on investment (ROI) or return on net assets (RONA), to express their earnings objectives. Further, most prefer to target RONA because it emphasizes line management's responsibility for the efficient use of all permanent invested capital (debt and equity) and because it allows the effect of debt leverage to be considered separately. Thus RONA has become the central element in management's effort to stimulate the flow of internally generated equity capital, the principal source of plannable funds.

The majority of the managers believed that the firm's "reach should exceed its grasp" in earnings as well as in sales. For the most part, their companies equalled or exceeded their competitors' average RONA performances, as Table 3-3 indicates. Yet these performance records were less a matter for self-congratulation than a base from which new earnings achievements were sought. In every case but one, management chose a target RONA that exceeded the company's average performance over the preceding eleven years. Its goals clearly challenged the organization to surpass both the industry and itself.

The derivation and modification of specific return on investment standards will be discussed at length in subsequent chapters. However, it is important to emphasize that management's practice differs significantly from the textbook process prescribed for formal capital budgeting or investment analysis. In the literature the return on investment criterion is derived from a measure of the corporate cost of capital because it is assumed that the enterprise can increase its—and its shareholders'—wealth only by equaling or exceeding that cost. In turn the cost of capital is derived from data on the going rate for equity and debt in the public capital market, with an appropriate allowance for risk differentials. Thus in theory management's target for the investment of internally generated funds should mirror the standards of the external capital market's standards. However, in practice the two are not identical, even if the company follows a formal capital-budgeting process with an established hurdle rate.

Table 3-3. Sample Data on RONA Targets and Performance

		Company RONA		Industry RONA	
		Target (%) (1978)	Average Actual Performance (%) (1968–1978)	Selected Competitors	
Company				Mean (%)	Range (%)
Technical	I	18	16.3	NA	NA
Products	II	14	10.6	10.0	8.3–11.3
	III	17	11.2	10.0	8.2–14.0
Consumer	I	27	14.9	NA	NA
Products	II	14	12.7	13.3	12.3–17.9
	III	14	16.3	15.8	10.3–23.0
	IV	19	11.0	10.3	8.3–14.1
Commodity	I	18	8.4	12.7	7.6–16.3
Products	II	Best in Industry	7.2	NA	NA
	III	13	8.6	8.9	7.3–10.0
Conglomerate	I	16	12.4	10.3	7.8–12.4
	II	9	8.6	10.3	7.8–12.4

Note. Calculation of After-tax RONA: $\dfrac{\text{Net PBSI } (1-t) + i\,(1-t)}{\text{Total Tangible Assets } - \text{ Current Liabilities}}$

PBSI = Profit Before Special Items

The difference primarily arises because of the distinction between an ongoing investment process based on a commitment to meet or exceed a standard and a process that implies intervention and/or interruption whenever failure to meet the standard is anticipated. In other words, it is the difference between management and measurement, between the coach and the referee.

The natural complement of management's target RONA is its target for dividends (Table 3-4). In this regard the research study uncovered no real surprises to well-established views of corporate dividend policy. Top management teams recognized the importance of dividends as a signal of financial well-being and as a measure of cash-flow volatility. They knew that unexpected discontinuities conveyed a disconcerting prospect of a management surprised by events and not in full control. Consequently they stressed the importance of dividend continuity and emphasized strongly the need for growth to keep pace with earnings and general inflation. However, as these managers thought about dividend policy they were concerned less directly with their shareholders than with the flow of funds within the firm. Thus they concentrated on dividend payout targets instead of dividends per share.

As is readily apparent, dividend payouts are the obverse of retained earnings: those earnings or cash flows which are not distributed will be available for corporate reinvestment. A dividend policy expressed in terms of a payout rate could be expressed equally well as an earnings re-

Table 3-4. Sample Data on Dividend Payout Ratios

Company		Company Ratios		Industry Ratios	
				Selected Competitors	
		Target (%) (1978)	Average Actual Performance (%) (1968–1978)	Mean (%)	Range (%)
Technical	I	Nominal	12	15	5–22
Products	II	33	47	42	32–65
	III	Below 50	62	58	49–63
Consumer	I	Flexible	26	39	18–52
Products	II	35–40	34	39	21–62
	III	33 Inflation Adjusted	54	52	46–57
	IV	50–55	56	39	23–51
Commodity	I	30–40	46	52	48–54
Products	II	50–55	55	52	44–57
	III	30	57	54	48–61
Conglomerate	I	40	41	27	0–50
	II	25	21	27	0–50

tention policy. The implications of this orientation are apparent in the financial planning documents of a company whose profit margins were below the *Fortune* 500 average. From the shareholders' perspective, it would be reasonable to assume that the company's payout would be inversely proportional to its profitability, on the theory that the better the earnings performance, the more justification and opportunity for reinvestment. In reality, the president argued just the reverse in a document circulated to his four top executives:

Objective #1   Increase the Return on Net Assets
   Our profit per dollar of sales is significantly below the average of the *Fortune* 500 industrial companies. Some of the basic causes are:
   mature industries;
   below-average new product innovation;
   below-average value added;
   cyclicality.
   Clearly, raising profit margins must be everybody's primary short-term objective. . . . Net asset turnover is also important. . . . While adequate return on investment is our ultimate objective . . . primary long-term emphasis must be on raising margins as a result of attaining increased market share except where unusual growth makes substantial increases automatic.

Objective #2   Increase Dividend
   A corporation's most important constituency is its shareholders. Studies have established that dividends, or the prospect of dividends, is in the end, the only real return shareholders receive. . . . It is our obligation to run the company so that its shareholders receive . . . tangible rewards in the present. (This will be reflected in the market value of the stock.)
   Our present policy is to pay out [X%] of aftertax earnings in dividends. While this is substantially lower than the annual average for all major corporations, *it is so by design. It reflects our less-than-average profit margin and cash flow, and the fact that we must preserve as much cash as possible to purchase improvement in our position* through high return, capital expenditure. (Emphasis added.)

   The line of reasoning expressed here is a very natural one for proactive organizational leadership to take: our performance is below average; it must and can be improved; we are confident of our ability to accomplish our goals; therefore, we are justified in asking our shareholders to make an above-average reinvestment of earnings to fund it. Such self-confident managers assume that the shareholders will agree with their optimistic views and, in time of need, they lean toward the highest acceptable target earnings-retention ratio consistent with the continuity of dividends per share. Indeed, these top managers generally preferred to keep their payouts as low as possible in the belief that "we can make better use of the money than our shareholders can," given reinvestment opportunities and the personal tax advantages of undistributed earnings. None sought to increase payouts as a deliberate policy. All spoke often about the need for a reasonable or fair dividend policy—thereby suggesting that in the absence of such concerns, internal pressures would result in lower payouts.

Individual definitions of a reasonable payout varied considerably, as Table 3-4 indicates. The companies' current targets ranged from 25 percent to 55 percent of earnings with an average of 38 percent. The study provided no evidence of an objective reasoning process by which these numbers were derived. Rather, the numbers appeared to originate in the level of corporate need, conditioned by past payout practices, the observation of payout levels among comparable companies, current market expectations (particularly in recent years as dividends have appeared to figure more prominently in stock selection), and—occasionally—the direct or indirect prodding of takeover initiatives which focused attention on shareholder reward.

Running throughout these considerations was the need to conform to the range of general practice; yet the range also offered considerable room for choice, without appearing to violate group norms. In general, the managers were responding to pressure to adjust dividends per share to keep pace with inflation while simultaneously endeavoring to retain more of their earnings than they had in the past. Most companies' current targets called for reduced payouts, and only two exceeded their historical averages.

Before turning from dividends to debt, it is important to note that on this issue, as on other matters of financial policy, individual managers tended to reflect the viewpoint of the constituency with which they were most closely associated by reason of their organizational responsibilities. Differing viewpoints were often apparent within the same company, as the following comments demonstrate. Not surprisingly, the strongest concern for dividend payments was expressed by the company's chief financial officer who said:

> The most stringent financial policy is the dividend policy. We are determined *never* to cut the [absolute] dividend payment and seek to

increase it when trends justify. Our equity security represents a "bond equivalent" in the eyes of the shareholder. We take great pride in our dividend record—it's part of the corporate culture.

In contrast, a retired chief executive and current board member of the same company commented:

We have a commitment to good earnings—not to dividends. We used to think that a 50% payout was right but now the fashion is to pay less. I don't believe in paying out all the earnings to the shareholders, and 50% is a reasonable division. In bad years, I would favor reducing the dividend if necessary.

Clearly, his organizational identity and viewpoint persisted, despite the fact that he was now first and foremost a shareholder himself.

The third and last set of dominant supply-related financial goals relates to the use of debt as a source of permanent capital. For all but one of the companies, debt was an acceptable, if not desirable, source of long-term funds and a regular part of the corporate supply. In the case of the exception the zero debt target was a corporate objective which could be traced back to the founders' experience in the 1930s, when bankruptcies precipitated by default on debt contracts were common. To quote one of the founders, "What do you do with borrowed dollars? I think most of us believe something unwise."

Although most of the corporate managers were less extreme than this in their views, they shared a preference for debt policies they characterized as conservative. They pointed out that debt was easy to increase and hard to cut back. They recognized that debt limits were arbitrary, but they took comfort in a line which looked conservatively drawn. Debt was desirable in that it allowed them to grow at a faster rate, perhaps faster than the average; but too much debt deprived the company of its ability to meet unexpected needs and survive. Some managers expressed their thinking about a debt reserve in terms of avoiding circumstances in which "the next financing had to be equity."

As with dividend policy, these observations provided no surprises but confirmed the important role of debt in long-term financing strategy. The specific guidelines used reflect a position bounded by the norms of the industry and of the capital markets on the one hand, and the needs of the business on the other. Thus there tended to be less uniformity among the managers' debt practices than in their other supply-related goals. Nevertheless, these company policies were genuinely conservative. Where credit ratings were an explicit objective, management targeted ratings of A or better, which would allow a comfortable margin of safety by conventional standards. Debt/equity ratios were similarly set, so that debt would continue and grow only as equity grew through retained earnings.

As Table 3-5 indicates, these debt targets, or more accurately debt limits, ranged from zero to one dollar of long-term debt for each dollar of equity. In each case the target equaled or exceeded the company's ten-year average debt level, thereby tending to confirm the target as a limit which, with built-in repayment schedules, would produce the desired average results.

Corporate managers considered a variety of factors as they set these debt limits. Among them were: the needs of the business; the need for a substantial reserve for both offensive and defensive use; the use of debt by close competitors in the funding of competitive strategy; the opinions of the capital-market power centers—bankers, analysts, and credit rating agencies; and the managers' own subjective sense of the riskiness of any given amount of debt. The ultimate risk with which the managers were concerned was the loss of independence and control consequent upon falling into the hands of "those damn banks." As the executive who described the banks in these terms went on to say:

> They will cut you off and they will be cold-blooded as hell. I don't want to be in the position where our money market center can control me.

Table 3-5.   Sample Data on Debt-Equity Ratios (debt as a percentage of equity)

Company		Target (%) (1978)	Average Actual Performance (%) (1968–1978)	Selected Competitors	
				Mean (%)	Range (%)
Technical	I	Zero	Zero	12	7–15
Products	II	33 (AA)	22	31	13–52
	III	38 (AAA)	17	55	42–76
Consumer	I	Flexible	19	16	13–19
Products	II	82 (A)	75	45	8–72
	III	33	16	24	1–43
	IV	54	29	38	30–46
Commodity	I	67	23	26	10–42
Products	II	54 (AAA)	39	35	28–43
	III	54 (A)	52	43	35–48
Conglomerate	I	50	31	71	46–135
	II	100	68	71	46–135

Note. Target credit rating is given where applicable.

Listening to these comments, it is hard to remember that the speaker is a top executive in a large, mature, and profitable corporation—not a sidewalk entrepreneur. Yet many of his peers in other companies expressed the same concerns although they phrased them more elegantly. As the founder of one of the companies observed:

> If you sit in on our board meetings you would see how conservative we are. . . . I have this turmoil inside of me. Others borrow money and maybe we should [borrow more]. . . . We have two sets of influences here—those who lived through the Depression, and those who lived through '74–75 . . . are we too conservative? . . . When you move too far away from basic principles . . . you may be putting the future generations in a position that's dangerous. . . . There is no way in the present environment we can run [Name of Company] the way the analysts want us to run it. We've been in business for [over 100 years] and we want to be in business for another hundred.

Short of the extreme event of losing control, the value of a conservative debt limit was seen to lie in its ability to guarantee continued funding flexibility (through debt and equity) in the face of competitive uncertainty. Access to the capital markets *regardless of conditions* was the key consideration. Of course, the level of debt deemed conservative was to some degree a function of need and experience. New levels of debt brought on by urgent competitive spending priorities could and did become the new conservatism, if found to be tolerable over an extended period of time. However, beneath these judgments was management's abiding concern for organizational survival. As one executive remarked:

> The debt policy [of our company] reflects a primary emphasis on freedom—that if we maintain the debt limits we have set, we will be free from bank restrictions and the banks will not inhibit our activities. This, along with our earnings goals are *parts of the whole concept of a desirable quality of life* for management. (Emphasis added.)

In the following chapter we shall see how these concerns are realized through management's efforts to balance its financial goals system.

Notes

1. As used in this book, the term "strategic investment" refers to management's financial commitment to its major, ongoing productive activities. By con-

trast, "opportunistic investments" are those which represent the potential for a change in strategic direction. In the short run, at least, management has greater freedom to accept or reject these opportunities, because no organizational "stake" yet exists. As we shall see, investments that are initially opportunistic can, in time, become a vital part of the corporate income stream to which long-term commitments are made.

2. Michael E. Porter, *Competitive Strategy* (New York: The Free Press, 1980).

3. This assumption has been upset in recent years by the significant price discontinuities created by inflation. These distortions were a cause for serious concern at the time of this study, but a satisfactory inflation calculus had not yet been worked out. Financial goals statements continued to be formulated on the assumption of a relatively stable sales to assets relationship. The impact of inflation is discussed more fully in Chapters 5 and 8.

4. The role of equity in acquisitions for new product market initiatives is discussed in Chapter 8.

4

A Financial Goals System for
Established Product Markets

Setting Priorities

In the preceding chapters the modern industrial corporation has been described as an enterprise dependent upon multiple constituencies for its survival and the success of its business mission. These constituencies make distinctive demands on the firm through their representatives or sponsors within the top management team, and their interests can diverge significantly. Consequently, the potential for conflict among top management's financial goals always exists. As one senior officer observed:

> There is a continuing dialogue between the office of the chairman and the planning people. We have lots of financial goals, not all of which are compatible. So there is a continuing debate as to aspects of compatibility and which is to be ascendant—how rapidly can a private company afford to grow, particularly with a limit on utilization of debt . . . If we tried to optimize all our goals, we'd have a problem. As it is we fall into the trap of giving lots of emphasis to goals that do conflict with each other. . . .

Not all chairmen or chief executives will tolerate a "continuing debate" over the critical issue of corporate priorities, of course. However, on the face of it, there appears to be no reason why a number of aspirations could not coexist in a diverse partnership for extended periods of time without a confrontation. Growth and an acceptable return on investment, dividends and retained earnings, debt financing and reserve borrowing power, investment expenditures and profit, results now and results later—in principle, all could receive some degree of management's attention and record some degree of accomplishment.

The firm in which management seemed most inclined to take a laissez-faire attitude toward its financial goals was one of the consumer products companies. At the time of the study the company was enjoying a strong growth market for its primary proprietary (branded) product. This growth had continued for more than a decade, first domestically and later overseas. Management therefore had become accustomed to sustained rates of growth and rates of return well above average for the traditional industry and for the economy. In addition, the business was not capital intensive and management had ample resources at its disposal to fund the available growth. Hence it was self-confident and refused to be pinned down by external or internal performance standards. As the president commented, "We set our own par for whatever course we play on. There ain't no other company just like us."

Nevertheless, expectations and financial objectives did exist. The president expected his company to outperform at least three-quarters of the industry, and other executives shared his view. The company's financial officer expected that dividends would increase at a rate equal to or ahead of inflation, even though he declared that "we are unanimously opposed to having [a dividend payout policy]." Top management clearly intended to draw down as much debt as possible, short of being placed so that "one money market center could control us." But it refused to define a precise debt policy, lest its flexibility be limited.

Significantly, the management of this company was not opposed to using new equity issues to fund the growth of its established product market, and it had already done so on one occasion. As an executive commented, "It's easy to get equity money. Millions and millions are available if we wanted it. All you have to do is run a good road show." Translated into more tempered and professional terms, this apparently cavalier remark implies that the strong record of a strong company will speak for itself when brought to the attention of receptive investors. True as that assumption may be, however, it also should be noted in this connection that top management retained the ability to control a significant block of stock. Thus, as the chairman asserted, "We're still relatively safe from takeover if we stick together."

Top management's apparent indifference to the need for either a clear and concise statement of individual corporate and financial goals or some acknowledgment of corporate priorities can therefore be attributed to two related factors. The first is the company's sustained superior per-

formance in the industry (and economy); the second its abundant resources. Money was simply not an issue when the top managers reviewed
their investment options *at this stage* in the company's development.
Management talent was the resource which limited their choices, not the
supply of funds, as the chief of overseas operations indicated. "Funding
has never been a problem. . . . There are four criteria for a Go-No Go
decision: (1) Is it in our business? (2) Do we have the management manpower? (3) What is the political risk? (4) What's the potential ROE and is
the risk worth it?"

This company's experience was a rare exception among the group of
large, relatively mature enterprises included in the study, however. Most
of the other managements were keenly aware of their firms' financial and
competitive environments, and they were similarly alert to the potential
interdependence of the several financial goals they sought to pursue. (In
fact, despite its bravado, even this management was not entirely free to
ignore such concerns, as their policies indicated.)

The key to the interdependence among a company's financial goals
lies in the scarcity of corporate purchasing power (actual or perceived) by
which management implements its decisions. As has been seen, every financial goal can be classified in terms of its immediate impact on the flow
of funds within the firm. Some goals, chiefly those related to the competitive drives of the product market and to organizational well-being, define
the demand for funds. Others, chiefly those related to the capital markets, define their supply. Given an infinite supply of funds these relationships do not impinge on management's plans. If the supply of funds is
finite, however, as most of these top managers believed, then the demand
for funds does become a financial planning problem.

Readers versed in classical financial theory and traditional interpretations of American capitalism may be surprised by the notion that management's investment funds are limited. From traditional perspectives
the deep pockets of the American debt and equity markets are always
available to fund any appropriate investment by any company at any
time. The basic limitation on corporate growth is not the scarcity of
funds, therefore, but rather the scarcity of opportunities for profitable
investment (i.e., investment that promises a return equal to or in excess
of the market's cost of capital). In other words, the firm could get all the
capital it needed for the right opportunity and *at the right price.*

This last principle is the implicit assumption in all discounted cash
flow analyses. However, it was significantly qualified by the large majority of the managements studied during the period under review. Their

behavior conformed with an environment of capital scarcity rather than capital abundance. Why such behavior would appear rational has already been indicated in the preceding chapters. As has been seen, most managers give paramount importance to a reliable, predictable stream of funds to support vital competitive strategies and long-term organizational survival. External debt and equity markets are perceived as ill informed and untrustworthy, particularly in periods of heightened uncertainty. Self-sufficiency is given priority as the prerequisite of true independence, and line managers are disciplined by the insistence that they earn their own pocket money. Thus even the largest and most creditworthy industrial corporations function under the tight discipline of capital scarcity in funding existing product markets.

Once this discipline has been recognized, however, it also becomes apparent that the company's key financial goals are part of a comprehensive goals system which must be reconciled and balanced. An adjustment in one goal will inevitably require a compensatory adjustment elsewhere. A fundamental and persistent balance must be struck between demand-related and supply-related goals, just as actual funds flows must be balanced. Priorities among conflicting goals must be established so that critical tradeoffs can be made.

Management's conscious recognition of this interdependence has come to the fore only within the past ten to fifteen years, and even today it is neither universally understood nor accepted by all managers who play an important role in the allocation of funds. Prior to this, key financial goals tended to be fragmented and isolated from one another, as this corporate treasurer pointed out in recounting his company's experience:

> In 1971 we had a [management retreat] when it became obvious that the company's goals were inconsistent. Various people wanted:
>
> a 50% dividend payout
> no debt
> an increasing ROI
> to grow like crazy
>
> It was clear that we had to come up with a consistent set of financial policies.

In addition, goals were often presented in forms that masked inconsistencies and/or precluded reconciliation. Thus a goal of "5 percent to 8 percent growth in sales, inflation adjusted" could safely coexist with a goal of "improving return on assets," and a goal of "15 percent ROI, company-wide," could persist—uneasily—alongside a goal of "market leadership: be number one in market segment."

Now, however, most managements accept the interdependence of key financial goals as a basic premise in their strategic thinking and planning. Discussions with top managers about the origins of particular performance criteria reveal their awareness of the need for balance in the flow of funds. They also reflect the tradeoffs and compromises among competing goals which must be made as a corporate financial plan takes shape. Indeed, the latter is an inevitable focal point for internal struggles over scarce resources, as the managers seek to reconcile their goals and their expectations.

Representative comments from the managers of several companies illustrate the ways in which these interrelationships are worked out in financial plans. In addition, they give the reader a sense of the competitive mind set apt to appear as top managers adjust established product-market strategies to the constraints of a finite internal capital market. First we listen to a board chairman and his treasurer discuss their corporate goals:

> In the early 1970s we had a top management conference and we articulated three basic objectives: to become a large company by the early 1980s, to be an industry leader and to achieve a 15% ROI. . . . The answer to the origin of the 15% target is that we backed into it. We started by asking what we had to invest to achieve the desired growth and then asked what did we have to earn [to fund that growth] without pulling rabbits out of a hat.

> In 1972 we put three young MBAs on a computer study of scenarios of growth versus capital intensity. We determined that a "Premier Company" would earn 15% ROI (from *Forbes* and *Fortune* 500 data). From this we did sustainable growth rates which turned out to be 12% to 13%. We decided to preserve our AA rating. Dividend rates followed. The historic payout was tied to the growth rate.

A chief financial officer explains some of the strategic consequences his company's goals entail:

> We know we can do 4% on net sales. We know that with that return we can grow at 10% to 12% and still pay dividends. We know this as a fact and don't have to have a computer to find it out. But we expect

our people to do 6% to 8% on sales in which case we can grow at 20%. If we don't achieve 6% to 8% in sales then the pressure is on management to get it there, not on the financial office to find the funds [for growth]. We keep the heat on operating management and don't let them off the hook by resorting to other financing.

And finally, a chief planning officer reflects on the tradeoffs he and his colleagues had to make to ensure a sufficient supply of internal capital:

Historically we had a dividend payout target of [above 50%] which was very high. In the last few years it has been reduced. We have gone through all kinds of numbers to show the necessary capital formation in order to support the desired corporate growth rate. There is no way we could compete for market share and continue to pay out [above 50%] of our earnings. Even a 50% payout is questionable. The dividend policy is the most sensitive part of the calculation. . . . It is the [CEO's] position that the company needs an X% net income on gross assets if it is going to sustain the desired corporate growth rate.

Interestingly, this last executive went on to comment about the possibility of a capital shortage in the country at large (then a much-debated topic). He believed that no such shortage would occur, "because the economy will simply slow down. In other words, companies will simply finance whatever growth they can finance and stop there." Other top managements' financial practices tended to support his belief. They made the concept of self-sustaining growth in established product markets a central part of their financial planning.

The Self-Sustaining Goals System

The propositions which influence the managers of mature industrial corporations as they set financial goals for established product-market positions have already been discussed. In summary they are as follows:

- At any given period every enterprise has a defined business mission which is realized in its established competitive positions in particular product markets. Corporate strategy centers on these competitive positions.

- This strategy may include a harvesting mode for a few mature and relatively unprofitable business units. But for most of the firm's product markets it is designed to maintain an existing market position or expand that position against primary competitors.

- Competitive strategy therefore dictates that the firm grow at least as rapidly as aggregate industry demand grows. The firm's targeted growth rate of sales must meet (or exceed) the expected growth rate of the industry, and its growth rate of investment must keep pace with the growth rate of sales if the competitive strategy is to retain its credibility.

- Thus the firm's financial goals system receives its initial impetus from without—from the economic and competitive environment of its established product markets. Management can disengage from this momentum only by abandoning either particular product markets or its commitment to competitive excellence (defined as parity or superiority). Moreover its freedom is shortlived: to abandon one product-market's discipline is to adopt the discipline of another.

- To achieve equilibrium in the financial goals system the aggregate supply of funds must be equal to the demand. Thus the inflow of funds implicit in the firm's rate of return targets must be equal to the outflow implicit in its target growth rate of sales.

This last proposition can be expressed by a simple mathematical equation, known in the academic literature as a self-sustaining growth equation. The equation includes all the principal elements of a financial goals system for an established product market plus a figure which reflects the company's expected after-tax interest rate on outstanding debt. Thus it is composed of the following elements (listed with the symbols that represent them in the equation):

- The company's growth rate of sales, or $g(S)$

- The company's return on investment (using the common Return on Net Assets), or $RONA$

- The earnings retention ratio (the complement of the dividend payout target), or r

- The debt-to-equity ratio, or d

- The expected after-tax interest rate, or i.

By limiting management's primary financial goals to these objectives, we assume that in the long run it will be able to fund the growth of mature product markets from retained earnings, supplemented only by a conservative amount of debt (that is, debt defined as a constant proportion of growth in equity). In fact this was management's dominant assumption in the large majority of these industrial corporations. Thus it follows that their goals were designed to constitute a self-sustaining system, and that this system was accurately reflected in the self-sustaining growth equation:

$$g(S) = r [RONA + d (RONA - i)]$$

Two points should be made here, lest the reader fear that we have suddenly withdrawn from corporate reality into academic theory. First, the managers themselves spoke clearly about the interdependence of financial goals, as the comments cited earlier indicate. Indeed, they were particularly emphatic about the continuing tension between targeted growth on the left-hand side of the equation and targeted return on investment on the right. Second and more significantly, one or another variant of the self-sustaining growth equation was used by five of these managements to test the consistency of their individual goals systems. (See Table 4-1 for these equations.) Such usage attests to the practical significance of the equation and, more importantly, to the fact that management saw these particular goals as a tightly integrated system.

The self-sustaining growth equation for a balanced financial goals system can also be expressed graphically, as Figures 4-1 and 4-2 demonstrate. Here the equation is represented by a line defining those pairs of growth rates and rates of return on investment which will provide a rough balance in the inflow and outflow of funds, given the firm's targeted debt and dividend policies. (Pairs of goals which do not fall on the line will produce either a surplus or a deficit of funds.) For example, Figure 4-1 shows the paired goals for a company in which management neither borrows nor pays cash dividends. This is an unusual case, but one such company, Technical Products I, was included in the research sample. As Table 4-1 indicates, this company's self-sustaining growth equation is $g(S) = ROEq$. With neither permanent debt nor dividends, the company's Return on Net Assets is identical to its Return on Equity, and the system will be self-funding if the growth rate equals but does not exceed the rate of Return on Equity.

Figure 4-2 shows a more typical financial situation for a large, mature industrial firm. Here the company has some permanent debt and pays some dividends. As in Figure 4-1, these policies define the slope of the line that represents self-sustaining growth. But in this case the slope is necessarily less than 45°. Thus the appropriate growth rate for any given

Table 4-1. Self-Sustaining Growth Equations in Use by Research Sample Companies

Technical Products I $\quad g(S) = ROEq$

Commodity Products I† $\quad RONA = f[g(S)] + i^*$

Consumer Products III

$$g(S) = \dfrac{\dfrac{Net\ Profit}{Sales} - \dfrac{Dividends}{Sales} + d\left(\dfrac{Net\ Profit}{Sales} - \dfrac{Dividends}{Sales}\right)}{\dfrac{Fixed\ Assets}{Sales} + \dfrac{Net\ Working\ Capital}{Sales}}$$

Technical Products II‡ $\quad g(S) = d(RONA - i)(1 - p) + RONA\,(1 - p)$

Commodity Products III $\quad g(S) = r[d(RONA - i) + RONA]$

Note: Each of these variations could be readily converted into the standard form used in this study because each is a simple linear equation involving the same goals and ratios described in the text. In the list above, the symbols used in the text have replaced the company's symbols for identical variables where appropriate.

† $f = \dfrac{Eq}{NA}$ and $i^* =$ the added rate of $RONA$ needed to cover interest plus cash dividends

‡ $p =$ dividend payout

Figure 4:1   The Self-Sustaining Goals System Without Debt or Dividends

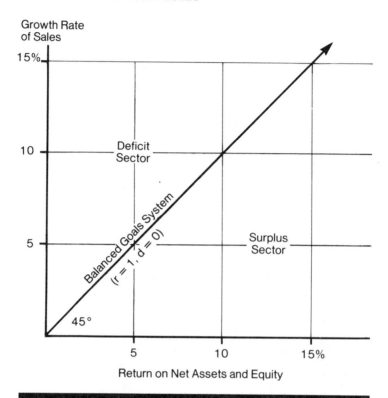

Note: r = Earnings Retention Ratio
      d = Debt/Equity Ratio

RONA consistent with self-sufficiency will be lower than it is in a company in which retained earnings are not reduced by debt repayments or dividends. In this case, for example, a 10 percent RONA will fund a 7 percent growth rate of sales, whereas it will fund a 10 percent growth rate in the no debt, no dividend case. The full range of combinations of growth rate, RONA, debt level, and dividend payout under the principle of self-sufficiency can be expressed in tabular form, as illustrated in Appendix A. Such tables, incorporating the unique circumstances of the individual company, can be readily developed as a useful planning tool.

Figure 4:2 The Self-Sustaining Goals System With Debt and Dividends

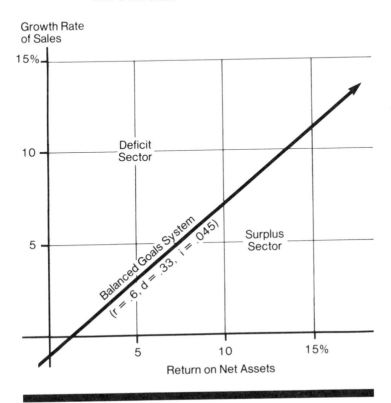

Note: r = Earnings Retention Ratio
d = Debt/Equity Ratio
i = After Tax Interest Rate

These graphic representations make it clear that the objective of self-sufficiency can be satisfied by an infinite number of growth and return on investment combinations. Goals systems represented by points farthest along the line to the right are the most aggressive. But given a company's existing debt and dividend objectives, any pair along the line could be chosen. To put the point somewhat differently, the desire to be financially self-sufficient requires management to define its financial goals system precisely, but it does not, by itself, define the particular goals to be included in the system.

Formulating the Self-Sustaining Goals System:
Some Underlying Assumptions

The form of the self-sustaining goals system may be somewhat puzzling to a reader with experience in financial analysis. The logic in equating $RONA$ and $g(S)$, rather than $RONA$ and $g(NA)$, is not immediately obvious, nor do the goals as stated relate directly to the actual flow of funds or purchasing power. Instead they appear to be an odd mixture of income statement, balance sheet, and cash flow ratios. What explains these apparent inconsistencies?

Two considerations account for the form in which these goals appear in the self-sustaining system. The first has to do with the general nature of financial goals, the second with their usefulness as a meaningful discipline on management: As virtually every manager recognizes, financial goals are never more than rough approximations. Ballpark figures represent management's best estimate of the firm's potential—what it would like to accomplish during the planning period. Further, if these goals are to discipline management's choices, they must be recognized and accepted as a reasonable measure of performance by those who must live under their discipline. Hence it makes good sense to use familiar income statement and balance sheet terms which have the appearance (though not always the reality) of objectivity and consistency. In this regard more precise, but also more obscure, funds-flow terminology would not serve as well.

And yet these accounting relationships and ratios are only proxies for the actual inflows and outflows of funds that are central to the management of corporate wealth. An increase in reported assets does not necessarily mean that funds have been expended during an accounting period; nor does an increase in reported revenue necessarily involve an actual receipt of funds. Thus the reader may be concerned that the goals as stated do not accurately measure the flow of resources to be managed. While there are circumstances under which this concern would be justified, in most cases these goals are appropriate proxies for funds flows. In practice financial goals represent management's average, long-term expectations with regard to rates of inflow and outflow. Therefore the actual rates may vary somewhat from period to period without violating those expectations. In addition, a set of leads and lags is built into receipt and expenditure reporting by accrual accounting principles and these tend to remain relatively unchanged over long periods of accounting practice. In normal periods, therefore, rates of flow in reported income will be mirrored by similar rates of flow in funds generated from operations. (Sudden changes in accounting practice or major discontinuities in the level of corporate operations could distort the goals system temporarily, of course. But if this happened, top management should be fully aware of the fact and its implications.)

Another problematic assumption implicit in the goals system concerns the relation of assets to sales. As the reader will see, the equation assumes that the growth rate of assets equals the growth rate of sales. Obviously this is not always the case, as companies may use assets more or less efficiently at different times and thereby alter the ratio. Improvements in the use of invested capital to support given levels of business activity, for example, would allow an increase in sales without a comparable increase in RONA. However there are limits to such improvements, and a well-managed firm would be expected to maintain a relatively stable ratio of sales to assets under normal circumstances. In fact, many managements do make this assumption for planning purposes, as Table 3-2 indicated, even as they are alert for major discontinuities which would require adjustments.

Thus far the problems inherent in the self-sustaining goals system have been readily addressed. However, one critical area remains to be explored: the refunding of a business' existing investment base. The self-sustaining goals system focuses on the funding of new or incremental investments related to growth. It does not concern itself with expenditures necessary to replace the existing assets which sustain current operations and upon which growth is based. To the extent that this question is addressed, the goals system as stated assumes that the internal funds flow represented by annual depreciation and amortization charges to the income statement will be adequate to cover all necessary annual expenditures. This is a reasonable assumption as long as the process of replacing existing investments is reasonably continuous and evenly distributed over time and the inflation rate is modest and steady.

The first consideration typically holds true in replacing working capital, but it is less likely to be the case in capital-intensive industries in which productive capacity is replaced irregularly and in large, inseparable increments. In such industries the replacement process cannot be continuous because major expenditures are one-time items, governed by the rate of technological change, competitive initiatives, and market strategies. Thus for any given five-year planning horizon, the inflow measured by depreciation charges may be wholly inadequate to cover necessary replacement expenditures.

The importance of the second consideration will be apparent to anyone who has followed the economy in recent years. The sudden and unexpected surge in the inflation rate, which began in 1974, has been so severe that it has created short-term working-capital problems for many companies, as well as major discontinuities in the cost of capital assets. As a result, inflation has raised serious questions about the efficacy of the self-sustaining goals system in its simple form. These questions have not gone unnoticed by the managements involved in this study, and their implications will be discussed hereafter. At a minimum they would seem to require an additional term in the equation to take account of an "inflation surcharge."

These useful qualifications notwithstanding, the self-sustaining goals system provides management with an invaluable funds-flow tool. Because it captures the principal components of funds-flow management and defines their basic relationships to one another, it enables management to identify the principal pressure points within its financial goals system. It also relates those pressure points to the constituencies from which they emanate and allows management to consider their impact on the allocation of strategic resources.

The Role of Reserves

Among management's strategic resources are its reserves, the pool of uninvested purchasing power represented by liquid assets, unused debt capacity, and reversible budget commitments (or discretionary expenditures). These reserves can be a critical element in funds-flow management, yet they appear in neither the financial goals system nor the self-sustaining growth equation. It is appropriate to ask why not.

In its simplest and most literal form, the self-sustaining growth equation says that there is a direct and inflexible connection between a company's rate of growth and its rate of return. Two consequences necessarily follow therefore. First, given the company's debt and dividend policies, it can grow no faster than its realized *RONA* permits. (In other words, its growth must fall along the line Figure 4-2 illustrates.) Second, given a competitive strategy defined in terms of share of market or rank in industry, the company must realize a specific *RONA* to sustain that strategy.

Management can seek corporate growth at a rate in excess of that stipulated by its funding policies and the company's realized rate of return. But it will be unable to bear the consequent funds-flow deficit unless it has substantial reserves of uninvested purchasing power. Judging by the experience of the research sample, this is a realistic possibility for mature companies *in the short run*. Under normal circumstances each of these companies operated at less than full financial capacity and its management was therefore able to sustain a strategy even though its key goals for $g(S)$ and *RONA* fell above the self-sustaining growth line. However, it was also clear that these managements rarely made the level or form of the reserves an explicit component of the financial goals system.

On the contrary, reserves were usually seen as a private resource, available only to the chief financial officer and/or the chief executive. Their size and potential disposition were rarely specified in advance, and they were deployed outside the formal planning process. Thus they were treated in a manner consistent with top management's belief that they provided a buffer between its expectations and plans on the one hand and reality on the other. In essence, reserves were to be played out at top management's discretion to insulate corporate strategy from incompatible experiences for some finite period of time. Were the reserves to be included in the goals system—and thereby seemingly committed to one or another formal strategic goal—this flexibility would be lost. In addition, the pressure on subordinate managers to achieve their goals would be materially lessened, because the managers would count on receiving assistance from the reserves should it become necessary. Thus it follows logically that top management holds reserves apart from its formal goals system and requires its organization to live by the system's assumptions.

Consistency in Financial Goals: Practice or Promise?

Although we have heard top managers testify to the interdependence of their financial goals, we have yet to ask whether their practice follows their pronouncements. Did the research companies' financial goals reflect internally consistent comprehensive systems, within the limits of a finite capital market and the principle of self-sustaining growth? Or was top management's desire for consistency and self-sufficiency more theoretical than real?

By applying the self-sustaining growth equation to the data obtained in the field study, we can answer this question for nine of the twelve companies.[1] The test is a simple and straightforward one, as an example will demonstrate. First the terms of the self-sustaining growth equation are replaced by the company's key financial goals with one exception: either RONA or the growth rate of sales [g(S)] is omitted. Then the equation is solved for the missing term, thereby generating the value (or implicit goal as it is called hereafter) which would bring the company's goals into balance. Finally, management's actual goal can be compared with this implicit goal, and consistency—or the absence thereof—can be quickly ascertained.

Our example draws on the financial goals developed by the management of Consumer Products II. As Table 4-2 indicates, the company's current target growth rate of sales was 12 percent, its target RONA 14 percent. Given an earnings-retention ratio of .65, a debt/equity ratio of .82, and an expected after-tax interest rate of 4.5 percent, were these goals consistent? When we solve for an unknown RONA, we discover that the company's implicit goal was 12 percent rather than the targeted 14 percent. Thus management's actual goal was designed to produce a modest surplus of funds:

$$g(S) = r[RONA + d (RONA - i)]$$

$$.12 = .65 [RONA + .82 (RONA - .045)]$$

$$RONA = .122$$

Similarly, management's implicit goal for growth works out to be 14 percent, whereas its actual goal was 12 percent. Thus strict consistency would suggest a reversal of these numerical goals. And yet, it should also be noted that management's actual goals are very close to those required to provide financial self-sufficiency in established product markets. Therefore the practical difference is slight, particularly when the approximate nature of all goals is taken into account.

Table 4-2 presents the results of these tests for internal consistency under the line item "implicit g(S)" and "implicit RONA." (An asterisk has been used to differentiate this term from the company's actual goal, e.g. g(S)* versus g(S).) On this evidence the nine companies with complete financial goals systems can be divided into three subsets. In the first set, the companies' key goals are essentially consistent. In the second they are moderately inconsistent. In the third there is a wide discrepancy between them.

The five companies with consistent financial goals systems were Consumer Products II and IV, Conglomerate II, and Commodity Prod-

Table 4-2. Financial Goals and Tests of Internal Consistency

Company		Current Financial Goals				Implicit Goals		Average Actual Performance (1968–78)			
		g(S)	RONA	r	d	g(S)*	RONA*	g(S)	RONA	r	d
Technical Products	I	NA	18	NA	Zero	18	NA	20	16.3	88	Zero
	II	15	14	67	33	11	17	9.8	10.6	53	22
	III	8	17	50	38	11	13	11.0	11.2	38	17
Consumer Products	I	17	27	NA	Flexible	NA	NA	18.0	14.9	74	19
	II	12	14	65	82	14	12	15.5	12.7	66	75
	III	15	14	67	33	11	18	15.1	16.3	46	16
	IV	14	19	48	54	13	20	11.9	11.0	44	29
Commodity Products	I	15	18	65	67	17	16	11.5	8.4	54	23
	II	NA	Best in Industry	52	54	NA	NA	11.5	7.2	45	39
Conglomerate	III	10	13	70	54	12	11	9.3	8.6	43	52
	I	8	16	60	50	13	10	7.5	12.4	59	31
	II	10	9	75	100	10	9	7.2	8.6	79	68

Note. g(S) = Growth Rate of Sales (%)
      RONA = Return on Net Assets (%)
        r = Earnings-Retention Ratio (%)
        d = Debt-Equity Ratio (%)

ucts I and III. In these companies management's current financial targets for $g(S)$ and $RONA$ fell within a range of ± two percentage points compared to its implicit goals. This range could ordinarily be accommodated by reasonable adjustments in the earnings-retention ratio or the debt-equity ratio.

In three other companies (Technical Products II and III, and Consumer Products III) the range between management's actual goals and its implicit goals was wider: ± two to four percentage points. In these companies the credibility of the targets for $g(S)$ and $RONA$ must be examined more carefully to determine whether the goals are in fact attainable under the circumstances of the particular case. For example, Consumer Product II's $RONA$ target of 14 percent would fund a sustainable growth rate of sales of only 11 percent, whereas the company's actual target growth rate was 15 percent. It is possible, of course, that management could draw on underutilized debt capacity, earnings retention capacity, or redundant assets which collectively would have the potential to fund a higher rate of growth over some finite planning horizon. However, it must be recognized that these circumstances would represent a one-time opportunity which could not be sustained indefinitely.

Finally, there is the case presented by Conglomerate I. In this company the discrepancy between management's actual and implicit $g(S)$ and $RONA$ targets was very large (± 6 percent), and it cannot be explained by excess funding capacity. Other explanations are possible. It could be that management still sets its goals in organizational isolation, so that the issue of reconciliation or internal consistency does not arise. Or it could be that the managers have human and organizational considerations in mind which outweigh the need for consistency. (For example, they might have chosen to focus on one goal as their primary corporate objective and dramatized that choice by setting up an aggressive, even unrealistic, target, so that the organization would be stretched to its limit.)

However, in the context of this study, a third possibility is the most interesting. As it happens, this company is one of two in the sample with a corporate strategy largely, if not entirely, detached from an industry identity and heavily based on diversification. Typically such diversification is funded by common stock, offered in exchange for the stock of the acquired company. Thus the principle of self-sustaining growth may not be applied *at the corporate level*, because the limits of the private capital market are breached. During the diversification phase, at least, management's demand-related growth goals could be uncoupled from its supply-related goals and treated with a degree of independence.

It is curious that management's actual growth objective falls substantially below the rate its *RONA* objective implies, but two factors may explain this apparent incongruity. For one thing, this management has chosen to emphasize the need for better performance in absolute terms, with particular importance given to growth in the company's earnings per share. It has not stressed the importance of meeting specific growth and *RONA* targets which emanate from corporate headquarters. For another, the primary initiative for performance and performance standards originates at the divisional level. In a highly diversified company such as Conglomerate I, this fact tends to produce diversity of standards.

Putting the Numbers in Perspective

Graphs and equations such as those presented above provide the clearest statement of the key elements of an integrated financial goals system founded on the concept of self-sustaining growth. In addition, they make the inescapable interdependence of multiple goals and multiple constituencies apparent. And yet, there is a danger to stating these goals in the oversimplified form of an algebraic equation or a graph, because these statements lend an aura of scientific precision to strategic planning that simply does not fit the reality. Some chief executives may pride themselves on "managing by the numbers," but the large majority would surely reject this image of themselves. Therefore it is appropriate to end this chapter as it began—with the general principles which guide top managers as they direct the flow of new corporate wealth to maintain and expand established product-market positions.

Foremost among these principles is the need to consider the long-term implications of financial goals as carefully as the actual day-to-day flow of funds. Because the supply of dependable corporate wealth is finite, and because the competition for funds within the corporation is vigorous, management must give close consideration to the goals that drive the long-term demand for funds and their supply. Only in this way can it hope to avoid a major imbalance in future funds flows which could threaten strategic priorities.

Initially, of course, management's goals may be shaped by its concern for a particular constituency's needs and priorities. The shareholders' perceived interest in immediate income will influence dividend policy as will the capital market's interest in the company's price-earnings ratio. The conventions of a credit-rating agency such as Moody's or the terms of an outstanding debt contract will affect management's debt policy. Growth objectives are likely to originate in the industry's dynamics and particular competitors' activities. Rate of return objectives may be partially influenced by the company's past performance or by actual or anticipated interest rates.

But the process of goal formation does not stop here. Survival, continuity, and competitive achievement—top management's ultimate organizational objectives—affect each individual goal by directing that tradeoffs be made among them. Sooner or later debt and dividend policies must be reconciled with the business' urgent need for new purchasing power. Rate-of-return objectives run a gauntlet between the realities set by competition in specific product markets and the need for new funds to sustain competitive initiatives. Corporate growth objectives confront the reality of available, reliable funding. Thus the opportunity to gain a little in achieving one objective depends directly on the ability to give a little on another.

In stating that management must strike a continuous balance between demand-related and supply-related financial goals, this chapter makes an important—but limited—point. It is limited because it says nothing about the particular set of goals management ought to choose. In theory, at least, an infinite number of solutions will satisfy the self-sustaining growth equation, and an infinite number of points will fall on the funds-flow equilibrium line. Which set is most appropriate for a given company, at a given time, is by no means self-evident. The remainder of this study addresses this and other questions concerning the formulation of financial goals and the management of corporate wealth. We shall begin by considering the forces that cause management to change its financial goals.

Note

1. As previously indicated, three managements had not developed explicit goals which could be used to complete the funds-flow equation. Therefore it was impossible to test for consistency in these cases.

5

The Forces of Change

A Question of Serious Intent

The research sample clearly indicates the increasing importance of formal planning and goal setting in large American corporations over the past decade. But because of differences in personality and leadership style, the role of formal planning varies considerably from company to company and period to period. In some cases top executives value formal goals highly, and their influence on management's behavior is evident. In others the goals system is given less emphasis, and its influence is more difficult to track.

In the typical case the planning process is extensive. The company has a statement of business mission, a detailed strategic plan with a five-year horizon, a set of projected financial and funds-flow statements, and a variety of specific financial goals relating to the planning period. A high-level staff planning group coordinates the planning process and works with divisional and financial managers to integrate the entire organization's plans and responsibilities. Performance against plan is monitored on a regular basis, and management compensation is related, in some degree at least, to the achievement of divisional and corporate goals. Thus the company's efforts suggest that real meaning and serious intent back up its financial goals. Goals and goals systems appear to have an important influence on management's behavior, and it therefore seems reasonable to expect that changes in them will reflect a significant shift in management's thinking and future behavior.

Nevertheless, few, if any, managers live by the book. On the contrary, they prefer to allow considerable room for unplanned opportunities and future economic events. Therefore, most top managements take a position somewhere between strict adherence to plans and goals and total disregard for them (particularly when the goals relate to the utilization of scarce critical resources). There are those who argue that formal planning inhibits good management in an uncertain world;[1] but the more widely prevalent attitude is reflected in such familiar maxims as "the journey, not the arrival, matters" and "the reach should exceed the grasp." In other words, formal planning plays an important role in developing direction, motivation, and accomplishment; but it is not allowed to become disabling if the company comes up short for some reason, good or bad.

Under guidelines such as these, the failure to meet goals does not spell disaster, although no prudent management will ignore the consequences, particularly if the failure has been persistent. Instead the old plan will be replaced by a new one—along with a new sense of optimism about its potential. However, given the assumption of serious intent, it is also clear that substantial changes in the firm's central objectives will be neither casual nor frivolous. Rather, they will reflect management's changing perception of the opportunities and/or the economic realities on which the firm's survival depends. Thus it is particularly important to examine the circumstances under which corporate goals change so that we may better understand their origins, their interaction, and the realities that shape and refine goals over time.

The Natural Resistance to Change

Once organizational goals or objectives are established they remain stable over time, for reasons inherent in their managerial function. Collective effort toward a difficult accomplishment requires consistent, well-understood guidance. Goals that are constantly changing are apt to be regarded as capricious and arbitrary, the product of weak or ineffective leadership. Thus, right or wrong, goals are likely to stay in place for an extended period of time, once they have been established and announced.

Customarily this extended period will last at least five years. This is the interval usually chosen for formal long-range planning, and it would be surprising if long-term goals could be accurately assessed in a shorter period of time, given that the performance of most businesses fluctuates considerably from year to year, and that it takes several years for persuasive evidence of trends to become apparent. In addition, management's judgment of corporate performance is always poised between the recorded past and the unrecorded future—a reasonable position given the common assumption that its control and influence will play a large part in transforming expectations into results.

The nature of the goals-setting process also accounts for the stability of established objectives. Corporate plans and expectations are not created by a single superior thinker who imposes his or her will on a submissive organization. On the contrary, they represent a negotiated consensus, usually achieved only with a great deal of time and effort. Often this time is regarded as unproductive because it is time taken away from the company's profit-making activities. Consequently, the organization must feel a real sense of urgency about reexamining its priorities, and it must have the will to sustain the stress and compromise of personal goals this process inevitably involves. Anyone who has ever been involved in such consensus building knows that it takes months (or even years) to accomplish and that few, if any, of the participants have an appetite for repeating the experience very soon. Unless circumstances or events force a confrontation, management naturally will be inclined to buy more time for a new direction to become apparent.

Finally, it is worth remembering that the success or failure of any goals system is personal as well as organizational. Every new statement or corporate direction will be characterized as a significant departure from the past (with which present management is intimately associated). It cannot succeed unless the corporate leadership is clearly and unequivocally committed to the new plan and determined to make it work. Yet the managers identified with a particular goal or goals may be very reluctant to admit defeat.

Given these considerations, it is not surprising to find powerful forces at work when significant change occurs. Usually they are forces that have been building for some time, before they are released by a particular event or trigger. Thus it is useful to recognize that the specific timing of a change often depends on events such as organizational or economic discontinuities which are themselves unrelated to the formal planning or goal-setting process. However, because they make a break with the past highly visible, they provide management with a convenient excuse to reexamine its priorities—if it is disposed to do so.

Finally, one last observation is in order before concluding this discussion of organizational inertia. As we have seen, management's ultimate organizational and managerial objectives are concerned with survival, independence, self-sufficiency, and personal fulfillment or success—fundamental human priorities. What this study calls financial or corporate goals are therefore really means to those ends, and we must be careful not to confuse the two. In our observation, management's financial and corporate goals changed, but its ultimate objectives did not. Consequently, once it became apparent that specific goals were inconsistent with survival and organizational success, they were not allowed to remain in place, whatever the real costs in time, energy, and bruised egos.

The Evolution of Formal Planning

During the years under review strategic planning evolved into the comprehensive formal process now common at most large enterprises. In so doing it became a force for change in its own right, as one company's experience over a twenty-year period illustrates.[2] As we shall see, the process was necessarily one of trial and error, and there were many short-term (and short-lived) goals that disappeared as their inconsistencies or inutilities became apparent over time.

Back in the early 1960s management's primary demand-related goals centered on absolute growth in sales. It aimed to double the company's dollars in some unspecified time. It also had a specific target for the rate of return on sales and a vaguely defined objective for return on investment. A target growth rate of sales appeared at about the middle of the decade along with a similar target for earnings growth. Inferentially these targets implied that sales would double in approximately eight years and that the company's return on sales would be stable. However, a target gross margin for the return on sales was the only formal definition these objectives were given. (This was also the one and only time gross margin was specified in the formal planning process.)

The next change in the goals system occurred in 1970, when management defined a new and much more ambitious corporate growth objective. Having reached the $1-billion level, the company set its sights on reaching the $2-billion mark by 1980. The growth rate of sales would be "above average," a qualitative restatement which left room for variations in year-to-year performance records. But a specific target return on equity was instituted, to guard against the possibility that growth would be achieved at the cost of return. This relationship was identified even more precisely the following year, when the target return on equity was replaced by a target return on assets.

By 1972, the company had entered an aggressive growth-by-acquisition phase, and absolute objectives for aggregate sales volume were successively revised in 1972, 1973, and 1974. A goal for growth in earnings per share was announced in 1972, but it lasted for only one year. Target debt-equity and dividend-payout ratios, added in 1973, proved to be longer lived. Moreover, their adoption was particularly significant, because it meant that all the key elements in the integrated financial goals system had been defined in a form that made their integration manifest. Although the guidelines themselves may have figured in the informal planning process for some time, this was the first occasion on which the planners felt confident enough to identify the numbers in explicit cash flow projections.

By 1973, therefore, the maturity of the financial goals system was well advanced. Absolute dollar sales goals disappeared by 1977-78. And growth rate objectives were revised to reflect the impact of inflation during the same years. The growth rate of earnings target was set at a multiple of the growth rate in sales; the return on investment objective was increased, probably in response to management's uneasiness about the economy's effect on the firm's long-term purchasing power and competitive position; and dividend policy was adjusted in recognition of management's desire to keep the shareholders' purchasing power "whole."

This financial goals system life cycle was typical of those found in the research sample, although some companies showed more resistance to change than others. As formal planning (including long-term cash flow planning) became more thorough and comprehensive, and as it was better integrated into the fabric of management, the need for an articulated set of comprehensive financial goals also became apparent. Most of these companies responded to that need. By the end of the 1970s the key elements of the goals system were in place. From that point forward specific numbers would be changed in response to changes in the relevant economic and human variables the numbers were designed to reflect.

Changing Constituencies

A corporate financial goals system represents management's balanced response to the varied and sometimes conflicting priorities of the primary constituencies essential to the company's survival and success. Therefore it is logical that changes in the system are likely to occur when the composition of a constituent group is significantly altered. New pressures are brought to bear on the goals system, and they are apt to redirect management's attention, priorities, and specific targets. Three examples will illustrate this process: a change in the composition or priorities of the ownership group; a change in the mix of product markets and competitors; and a change in the makeup of top management itself.

Ownership in a large mature corporation often shifts so gradually that it is difficult to document its impact on financial goals. However, a sharper picture emerges when ownership is concentrated in family hands. In these companies changes were observable, when power shifted within the family group, or when a son succeeded his father. Accession to power clearly brought reordered priorities, although differentiating between the influences on a new CEO created by his professional responsibilities and those arising from his ownership position is difficult at best.

For eight of the twelve companies studied, the post-World War II period marked the end of family control. In its place professional self-perpetuating management corps were developed. Simultaneously, statements of corporate mission were broadened to recognize the company's responsibilities to its customers, employees, and society as well as to the shareholders. Cause-and-effect relationships between these two changes cannot be traced; nor do we suggest that the professional managers were more enlightened or socially sensitive than their predecessors. Instead the change in priorities simply reflected the new managers' recognition of the constituencies' power and their importance to corporate well-being and survival.

In the professionally managed corporation two shifts, or potential shifts, in the ownership group had important consequences for financial priorities. The first occurred when the proportion of shares held by passive, long-term, loyal shareholders fell and the proportion held by institutions and managed by professional portfolio managers rose. In general, the latter were thought to be unstable owners, focused only on short-term results, quarter-to-quarter earnings per share and price-earnings ratios, capital gains, and dividends. Thus a shift in this direction tended to cause a tilt in management's sensitivity to these investor-oriented results.

Similarly, the possibility of a takeover often prompted management to reorder its priorities considerably. Heightened concern for the efficient use of capital, elimination of redundant resources, and efforts to generate new momentum by acquisition and diversification were common responses to the threat of an imminent takeover. (Typically, management's sensitivity to these threats waxed and waned like the phases of the moon.)

Unfortunately, although beneficial in some degree, these responses were not always in the company's best long-term interest, particularly when they involved hasty acquisitions designed to make takeovers less attractive or more difficult. In one instance, for example, an acquisition proved to be a mistake almost from the start, and the company has been living with the consequences ever since. As might be expected, the best defense against a takeover was one that could not be activated overnight: a record of superior management with confirming results.

Changes in the product-market constituency also led to new priorities and numerical goals. This process was particularly evident among the companies whose identity shifted from single-industry to multiproduct enterprises during the study period. As new divisions emerged, each with its own performance standards, industry-specific measures had to give way to universal financial criteria. Hence it was common to find operating margins and turnover ratios being replaced as measures of corporate performance by return on investment, return on equity, and growth in earnings per share.

Other changes in overall strategy and specific goals were provoked by the accompanying shift in the company's industrial peer group. Indeed, these changes might require management to rethink its entire environment, as in the case of one company, which shifted from an industry in which it was the recognized leader and set the standard for others to emulate to a new industry in which another company took the dominant role.

And, finally, management had to spell out its priorities, as the emergence of distinctive corporate-level and divisional-level goals systems made internal conflicts increasingly likely. At the corporate level, as we have seen, the emphasis falls on a balanced funds flow. Thus corporate managers are most concerned with investment criteria appropriate for allocating capital among primary income streams and funding criteria designed to assure a continuous flow of funds. However, divisional managers have a much more specific and idiosyncratic set of priorities. Focused on a particular industry and particular competitors, they demand corporate funds to pursue their competitive goals aggressively. Under these circumstances, it is hardly surprising that formal planning and articulated goals became essential tools for top management.

The third and last set of constituent changes that produced new corporate priorities were those in top management, particularly the appointment of a new CEO. Understandably, these were also the circumstances in which cause and effect were most readily apparent. Timing could be easily identified, and attributions were readily forthcoming—from the CEO as well as from his subordinates. Moreover, it was common for a new CEO to articulate a set of corporate goals which would differentiate his term of office from his predecessor's and signal a new direction for the company. Growth, more efficient use of resources, better financial performance, new areas of investment, and diversification of the revenue streams are all attractive candidates for such reformulations. But recognizing that not all of them can be pursued at once, the new CEO can be expected to stress one or two priorities, at some inevitable cost to the other goals involved in the interrelated system.

Typically, too, the CEO's term in office is short enough to be dominated by factors other than his own agenda. In retrospect, at least, it is usually clear that the economic climate and the then-current phase of corporate history (including the particular product-market mix) play significant parts in determining which goal will be most actively pursued. Therefore insightful CEOs will often fit their priorities to the times and emphasize those aspects of the goals system that are most relevant to the circumstances and opportunities their terms present. If a board of directors is unusually prescient or lucky, it will choose as chief executive a person whose values, motivation, and personal objectives are appropriate to the particular stage through which the company is passing or about to pass. Leadership in innovative diversification, for example, calls on intellectual and personal attributes which differ considerably from those required for the period of integration and consolidation that invariably follows—and they are rarely found in the same person. Therefore it is vital that those responsible for choosing a new chief executive assess the company's needs over the next decade correctly, and that they match their candidates' personal strengths to the corporate priorities they perceive.

Changing Expectations

Goals and aspirations are always relative: to one's own past performance, to a respected competitor's current or expected performance, to the business environment in which the goals are achieved. Because each of these reference points is subject to change, goals which once were valid can become unrealistic or inappropriate. But if the change is gradual, it may be some time before the inconsistency becomes so apparent that a response is unavoidable. Conversely, sudden and substantial discontinuities are likely to spark changes that can clearly be identified with the revised expectations they provoke. Several such discontinuities occurred during the decade under review, including business recession, money market crises, the OPEC cost/price squeeze and the general inflation that accompanied it, and changing equity market preferences.

The general business recessions of 1969–70 and 1974–75 were by far the most visible force for change in financial goals. A recession challenges the entire system because growth and profits invariably decline sharply, and debt and dividend policies are likely to be under pressure as well. The company's goals seem unattainable and existing targets appear increasingly unrealistic.

Management's response to a recession often took several years to codify, as the pattern repeated in a number of companies demonstrates. Given the usual month-to-month and quarter-to-quarter variations in activity, the onset of a recession was difficult to recognize at the time. Then, once a recession had been recognized and acknowledged, considerable uncertainty remained as to its depth and duration. Therefore management was likely to put its long-range planning on hold, as it dealt with its first priority: the day-to-day operating and financial problems created by the downturn. Changing gears once a recovery was underway was similarly delayed for some months or quarters, because its timing and strength were equally difficult to confirm. Consequently, the company's long-range planning and goals were likely to be several years out of date before they were given a hard look. When we consider that a thorough review of such goals may take several quarters to conduct, we can understand why major financial restatements tended to appear about two years after a recession. Predictably, 1972 and 1977 were popular years for corporate goals revisions.

These reformulations often reflected more than just the revised expectations that had grown out of the recession. The process of formulating goals and strategy is time- and energy-consuming for the CEO who views it as a way to gain understanding, consensus, and commitment from key executives. Thus it is not likely to occur more than once every five years or so. In this context the recession may provide a convenient interruption in the flow of corporate experience which enables top management to challenge established viewpoints and set a new course.

The money market crises of 1974 and the early 1980s also played a significant role in the shaping and revision of corporate goals, by making the specter of limited access to the debt and equity markets distressingly real. Goals and expectations concerned with the supply of funds felt the most immediate impact, but in time the entire goals system was affected. Faced twice in a single decade with the prospect that the external capital-market window would be closed or restricted at critically important junctures, managements responded by reaffirming their distrust of outsiders. The crises reinforced top managements' conviction that self-sufficiency was an essential ingredient of their financial strategy, because the external capital markets could not always be relied upon for critical strategic-investment funds. They also strengthened their disposition to use long-term debt conservatively and to provide ample reserves of borrowing power.

A third environmental change with profound implications for individual goals and for the integrity of the self-sustaining goals system was the surge of inflation in the latter half of the 1970s. Before that time, annual inflation had been modest enough that managers felt no need to recognize it as a distinctive phenomenon in formulating their targets for growth and rate of return. However, the sudden surge in the inflation rate stimulated by OPEC created grave concerns, which were only intensified by the subsequent emergence of double-digit levels that gave every indication of being structural and sustained. Widespread reexamination of the adequacy of financial goals based on dollar values ensued, as the following excerpt from a talk by a senior financial officer at a corporate executive conference illustrates:

> In your individual RONA targets there is an allowance for inflation based on the inflation factor which was included in your sales growth projections. If inflation changes, your RONA target will change by about eight-tenths of the change in inflation, due to the assumption regarding desired debt ratios for existing operations. In terms of business strategy, there is only one answer to inflation, if we assume that assets are already being managed to optimum levels and that debt deployment and debt/equity ratios are as desired. This answer is to raise profitability sufficiently to cover the additional cash flow requirement which results from inflation. Each segment, product line, and item must be able to support the effect of inflation or else we are playing a losing game. There can be no favorites. With inflation your tracking mechanisms must sense its speed and acceleration or deceleration in relation to the lead time for revenue realization.
>
> In conclusion on managing inflation: Don't wait—price up immediately to recoup the extra cash investment which inflation imposes on net asset requirements. And insist that each product carry its own weight in covering inflation requirements.

Efforts to incorporate an explicit inflation factor into self-sustaining growth equations were only beginning in earnest at the time of this study. Hence, most managers continued to use the same formal goals that had been in place before the higher-level inflation began, while making subjective ad hoc adjustments in applying them. However, these accommodations did not solve the most serious problem created by this inflationary surge: funding the replacement of the existing asset base. When inflation rates are low, the cash flows hidden by depreciation charges are apt to be roughly equivalent to the replacement dollars required. But at higher levels it does not take many years before new assets cost twice their original cost—or more. Consequently, managers faced with the need to replace large concentrations of fixed assets may find themselves making difficult choices between new growth and essential reinvestments. As their self-sufficiency disappears, they may be forced to revise their growth objectives, their ROI expectations, or even the concept of self-sufficiency itself.

Capital-market expectations regarding appropriate debt and dividend payout levels are the last category of environmental changes influential during this period. Attitudes on both these issues were changing during the late 1970s and early 1980s, although it remains to be seen whether the changes were fundamental or temporary. The evidence suggests that the companies were moving in one direction, while the capital-market moved in the other. At the very time that the companies were seeking to raise debt-equity targets and lower dividend payouts because of inflation and other funding difficulties, the market was becoming uneasy about both. This unease was reflected on the debt side by higher interest rates, limited lines of credit, and shortened maturities, and on the equity side by investors' preference for companies with high and sustained dividend yields. So far as corporate goals were concerned, the evidence suggests that management continued to give priority to corporate needs, although it was quite aware of the changing capital-market environment. However, the final—and authoritative—chapter remains to be written in the financial record of the 1980s.

The Performance Gap

If corporate goals are to discipline an organization in any meaningful way, they must be perceived as being attainable within the planning horizon and experience must provide confirming results. Aggressive goals take time to achieve, of course, and managers understand that performance will be uneven and the path unsure. But when a persistent gap between a company's goals and its performance exists, one or the other must change, or credibility will be lost.

The experience of the companies included in this study ranged widely in this regard. At one extreme was a company which had not attained its target return on investment for more than a decade. At the other were companies which revised their objectives every several years, as goals were surpassed or, less frequently, proved unattainable.

The company with the most serious and persistent performance gap was in the midst of an extended secular depression, which had affected the entire industry. Thus reality justified the company's poor performance in some sense. But why no response from top management? Why was the company's existing strategy allowed to remain in place? An answer can be found in the fact that management saw the company as locked into the base industry by its huge specialized capital investment, its specialized work force, and its organization's one-industry identity. No real alternatives capable of sustaining the enterprise in its current state seemed to exist. But then why not recognize reality and set an ROI target consistent with the facts? The reason appeared to be management's reluctance to give up on a long-term future for the industry and the company, including a "reasonable" return on investment that could sustain revitalization and growth. Abandoning the goal would clearly signal defeat, and hope sprang eternal in breasts without alternatives. Nevertheless, the ROI goal had little immediate disciplinary or discretionary power, and it did not figure prominently in periodic reviews of the company's accomplishments. In essence it was a nostalgic reflection of the past and a wistful article of faith in the future.

This company's experience also reminds us that it can take a considerable length of time for the external environment to deal the corporation a critical blow. Nevertheless, external pressures will finally become irresistible if a company is caught between its need for funds and its inability to get them from reluctant investors and lenders who are increasingly tightfisted. Realistically, a company cannot survive in the long run unless it can generate enough resources to compete aggressively (including the funds for capital replacement and R&D). Thus the failure to earn an adequate return inadvertently becomes a divestiture process—with the possibility of achieving salvation through a favorable diversification-acquisition increasingly remote.

A different sort of performance gap existed for companies experiencing the heady excitement of rapid growth. Here goals were revised singly and as a group whenever serious inconsistencies developed. For example, during a ten-year period, one rapidly growing company revised its target return on sales six times, its return on equity three times, its debt-equity limit three times, its dividend-payout target seven times, its growth rate of sales four times, and its absolute sales objective six times. If goals were designed only to provide stability and continuity in corporate planning, these results would be a disaster. In fact, they reflect the persistently high level of achievement which is the planning system's chief objective. Goals are meant to be surpassed after all. Management's problem, if it could be called that, was twofold. First, the company's resources were so fully employed that the various components of the funds-flow equation required frequent fine-tuning to be kept in balance. And second, the company's growth had been so rapid that goals consistent with its actual experience had to be presented incrementally, lest they appear dauntingly high.

Most of the companies in the research sample fell between these two extremes. On some occasions numerical goals were revised to accord with the company's performance; on others they remained intact, and management's strategy and actions were revised in an attempt to close the gap. Because specific goals are usually relative (i.e., they represent *rates* of change or performance), and because specific target dates are usually not assigned, the goals in and of themselves do not typically trigger strategic reconsideration or revision. Instead they are part of a mosaic of concerns which come together in unpredictable ways when the proverbial last straw forces management to confront its performance failures.

Major strategic reviews are the most visible product of these confrontations. At such times, goals and strategies are reshaped around pivot points created by the few goals that survive intact. These may point the company toward new products or indicate that older income streams must be terminated. But whatever the particular new direction, it will be accompanied by considerable organizational upheaval out of which new commitments must grow.

The Funding Gap

Thus far, we have examined forces of change that are qualitative. They must be filtered through top management's attitudes and judgment in uncertain and unpredictable ways before they provoke actual changes. In contrast, a funding gap is a more tangible and immediate influence on financial goals because it threatens management's most vital corporate priority: the continuity and solvency of the organization itself.

As indicated previously, unless a company's financial goals form an internally consistent and self-sustaining system, management's energies are likely to be directed toward goals that cannot be sustained in the long run, because they lead to a persistent funds-flow deficit. Performance consistent with the goals can be sustained for some time, of course, if the organization contains underemployed resources. For example, a higher rate of growth in sales than the self-sustaining ROI appears to allow may be achieved if the company's actual level of debt is below target, and/or its dividend payout exceeds the target, and/or its ratio of sales to assets can be improved by the investment of excess cash, the better use of working capital, higher spontaneous credit, or the availability of excess productive capacity.

However, if all existing resources are fully employed at maximum efficiency, and all the slack in the goals system has been eliminated, then any inherent inconsistency between the targeted rate of growth and the targeted return on investment will become painfully apparent. Either growth will contract to a rate consistent with the attainable return on investment, or the concept of financial self-sufficiency will be abandoned and management will resort to a new infusion of equity capital from the outside. A third possibility does exist, of course: Management can persist in its pursuit of financial goals that are inconsistent with one another and with reality. However, such persistence soon strains the goals' credibility and management's as well.

The Inevitability of Change

Given the powerful forces working to modify individual goals and goals systems, the wonder is not that corporate goals change so often but, rather, that most managements can maintain sets of financial goals for a time as meaningful guides to long-term strategic planning. Change is inevitable, and the absence of change provokes questions about the realism of management's goals. For example, at one company the CEO ordered handsome desk ornaments for all his senior managers. Designed to display the company's target return on investment in prominent roman numerals, the ornaments were a daily reminder of a superordinate and timeless objective for the managers involved. But for outside observers they were more problematic: Did their prominence and permanence attest to the target's timeliness—or to its unattainability?

Like other human aspirations, corporate financial goals are rarely fully compatible with the actual environment in which they operate. The negotiating process which gives them their specific form is marked by approximation and compromise, and goals are almost always under pressure, having tilted too far in one direction or the other for the comfort of all who are concerned. In addition, the stability toward which goals point can never be fully attained—even though corporate management must assert that it exists in order to evoke the necessary commitment from its organization. Consequently, the seeds of resistance are always present, inside and outside the organization. Confidential and candid interviews invariably bring latent conflicts to the surface because management and the external constituencies with which it identifies are anything but monolithic, despite popular belief. Debt levels, immediate return on investment, long-term growth, shareholder concerns—all are matters for continuing debate among those who think that one or another occupies too much (or too little) of management's attention.

Change is also assured by the fact that any given financial goals system reflects the then current phase of the organization's life cycle. Like individuals, organizations and product markets go through a maturation process. The goals system that is appropriate for an infant industry or company will not suffice once it has matured, and the same holds true for product markets.[3] The companies studied for this book are all mature in the sense that they are large, financially sound, and have existed for a long time. Yet each had individual product markets central to the corporate income stream which were following their own evolutionary timetables and required appropriate recognition in the company's goals.

As these considerations make clear, an effective goals system is an integral part of the management process. Management's strategy cannot succeed unless its goals reflect the company's economic and competitive environment. And yet, management must also maintain a balance in the flow of corporate funds. Therefore it cannot satisfy every request for scarce corporate resources—however attractive the investment opportunities those requests represent. How management makes its allocations decisions and how its choices are influenced by the goals system will be explored in the chapter that follows.

Notes

1. H. Edward Wrapp, "Good Managers Don't Make Policy Decisions," *Harvard Business Review* 45 (September-October 1967): 91–99.

2. Here, as elsewhere in the chapter, the class names assigned to the study companies have been omitted.

3. The goals systems characteristic of infant industries or companies are discussed in Chapter 7.

6

Allocating Corporate Resources:
A Test of Management's Priorities

The most critical choices top management makes are those that allocate corporate resources among competing strategic investment opportunities. Typically several such opportunities will be vying for management's attention and commitment at any given time. Proposals will be circulating for research and development projects, marketing campaigns, and equipment purchases. Established product markets will require funds to sustain competitive strength and presence. New product markets will require funds to ensure equivalent corporate vigor in the future. How do top managers decide among these choices, and what priorities guide them? More particularly, what relation exists between strategic investment decisions and the financial goals system described in preceding chapters?

Answers to these questions are provided by two complementary bodies of data. The first is the decade-long financial record compiled for each company. This record includes the company's formal financial goals, performance data for its primary product-market income streams, and management's discretionary expenditures broken down by product markets. The second set of materials comes from interviews and documents relating to specific strategic-investment choices made by top management in each company in the recent past.

Predictably, neither set provides precise cause-and-effect evidence identifying specific triggers for management's accept/reject investment choices. No magic RONA figure or other such seemingly objective evidence emerges to explain particular decisions. However, the central assumptions of the financial goals system influence the complex and subjective investment process to a considerable degree. Management's commitment to organizational survival and its recognition that survival depends on multiple constituencies are crucial factors in allocations decisions. Additionally, these concepts provide an overall framework for strategic-investment choices which traditional investment analysis, proceeding on a project-by-project basis, has not as yet provided.

Strategic-Investment Choices and Financial Priorities

From the perspective of the middle managers responsible for them, every investment proposal looks special and unique. However, these same proposals tend to become part of a broader strategic framework when they are viewed from the top of the organization. In this framework three basic issues predominate. They are:

- The determination of the aggregate amount of discretionary capital to be committed during the finite planning period, or *funding strategy*.

- The determination of the operating scale for each product market consistent with its specific goals and with overall corporate objectives, or *competitive strategy*. (Operating scale determines the general level of financial support needed for productive capacity and working capital and hence the implicit share of discretionary resources allocated to each product market.)

- The determination of the specific product markets (strategic business units or income streams) that will make up the strategic portfolio, and the timing of entry and exit, or *business strategy*.

As management considers specific requests within this strategic framework, the question of growth versus return inevitably arises. It does so, in part, because growth and the profits from growth are not necessarily concurrent.[1] Thus the most basic tension is a function of management's time line: the more management is preoccupied by near-term results, the more likely it is to place RONA ahead of growth; conversely, the more management emphasizes future competitive strength and position, the more likely it is to perceive the sequence as growth now, RONA later. Of course the two cannot get far out of line at the aggregate level, if corporate self-sufficiency is to be achieved.

Should management wish to pursue a more aggressive growth policy than that the attainable RONA can adequately fund, it may begin to question the targets related to established debt and dividend policies. (As noted previously, these targets define the slope of the self-sustaining growth equation. Lowering the dividend payout or increasing the debt-equity ratio will therefore raise the slope of the line and open up the possibility of attaining both self-sufficiency and the desired growth.) Such questioning redirects management's view upward and outward. It emphasizes goals that are the prerogative of the chief financial officer, the chief executive, and the board of directors rather than the goals for which operating management is responsible (i.e., growth of sales and profitability). And it turns management's attention to the external capital market which must ratify any change by increasing its contribution to the firm's funds. Thus the internal tension between accepting slower growth or improving profit performance is replaced by the external tension arising from the need to negotiate with shareholders and/or lenders at the highest level.

Once management has focused on these protected priorities (with which corporate staff planners will rarely tinker), it must still make a choice between the debt or dividend route. In general, dividends per share are more sensitive than the dividend payout per se, and credit ratings are likewise more sensitive than the debt-equity ratio. Consequently, management can turn to these targets—and does, when strategic considerations make additional funds imperative. Further generalizations are risky, however, because management's choices involve complex rational and emotional considerations. Additionally, much will depend on management's feel for the market's response to overt policy shifts at the time and to the board's reaction to the perceived risks.

Funding Strategy: The Limits of Discretionary Spending

In planning vital strategic expenditures management requires predictable sources of funds over which it can exercise a high degree of control as to timing, amount, and use. Given the choice between unlimited and highly uncertain funds, and limited but far more certain ones, therefore, these managers typically preferred the latter. As we have seen, internally generated funds were the basis for their funding strategies in established product markets. And yet, a strategic opportunity or need is inherently unpredictable in its timing and amount. How, then, can management resolve the potential conflict between the irresistible force of strategic need and the immovable object of limited supply?

The answer to this question is found in the fact that neither term in the relation is absolutely fixed. Instead the determination of the total amount of discretionary expenditures for any given time period depends on an iterative process of accommodation, arbitrated by a dominant— and at times arbitrary—top management. On the one hand, the managers may choose to increase the funds available through strategies which include an increase in long-term debt or a decrease in dividend payout. On the other hand, they may decide to accommodate the demand for strategic investment funds to the existing supply. Which option is chosen will depend as much on the power and importance of particular constituencies and their internal spokesmen as it does on circumstance. In addition, it will necessarily reflect the experience, expectations, and ego of the individual who has the final say, because these priorities are personal as well as corporate.

Several examples will illustrate the way in which this process of accommodation works. Table 6-1 shows the ten-year funding pattern for two companies. During this period the management at Company A was pursuing a vigorous expansion strategy, reflected here in the capital expenditure figures. More volatile than earnings and rising at a steeper rate, these expenditures put pressure on year-to-year cash flows, despite the company's generally improving after-tax earnings record, and despite the fact that expenditures were held below 100 percent of total internally generated funds in every year but one.

Management drew on its borrowing capacity and dividend potential in responding to this pressure. As the table indicates, new long-term debt was issued twice during the ten years under review: once in 1970, to cover a temporary surge in capital expenditure, and again in 1975, to fund-out a prior buildup of short-term debt (thereby substantially restoring short-term debt liquidity and reopening lines of credit). Both issues left the company well within its target debt-equity ratio of .40 to 1, a significant consideration from management's perspective. Dividends provided less flexibility, given management's unwillingness to cut the dividend per share, even when poor earnings performance drove the payout ratio to .71 in 1970 and 1971. However, the managers were able to bring the payout back to target as earnings improved, and it was held within the target range thereafter, even as per share dividends increased after 1973.

Hidden from our view in these figures are management's efforts to limit or stretch out discretionary spending. By combining these efforts with the flexibility provided by debt and dividend policy guidelines, the managers could achieve a balanced flow of funds over the decade. Specific amounts of discretionary expenditure were similarly determined year by year, through a give-and-take process within the limits set by the company's financial goals system. Thus the ultimate limit on spending was set by the combination of the company's actual rates of return on investment and the debt and dividend guidelines to which individual decisions conformed.

Company B's experience over the same decade differed significantly, as Table 6-1 demonstrates. Earnings were much more volatile and the company had a lower long-term rate of growth. Predictably, therefore, capital expenditures were also more volatile in absolute amount and, particularly, as a percentage of internally generated funds. However, even substantial cutbacks were insufficient to alleviate the strain on the company's year-to-year cash flows and discretionary expenditures. Reserve debt capacity provided some assistance here, as it did at Company A. But the primary and most dramatic evidence of management's need to increase the supply of funds is found in its decision to suspend cash dividends for two years in 1971 and 1972. (Secondarily, of course, it is also apparent in the 1970 and 1975 debt issues, which pushed the company's debt-equity ratio up close to, but not over, its aggressive 1 to 1 target.)

Management's tradeoffs in the preceding examples were focused primarily on adjusting the supply of funds available for discretionary spending. A third company's experience during the same period illustrates the tradeoffs that can be made to accommodate the demand for strategic investment funds to the available supply. These tradeoffs include the redistribution of resources across discretionary expenditure categories (that is, marketing, research and development, and capital expenditures) and the redistribution of resources within categories across product lines. The net effect of such changes is to compromise the company's growth objective for some or all of the product lines, for the time being at least.

Company C experienced constant cash-flow tension during the ten years under review. This tension increased in 1971 and 1975, as it did for the other companies, because of downturns in the economy; but its fundamental causes were to be found in the company's strong and steady growth coupled with a lack of ready reserves and top management's disinclination to make use of long-term debt. To cope with cash-flow pressures, management shifted its pattern of discretionary allocations significantly

Table 6-1. Sample Funding Patterns

Company A	1978	1977	1976	1975	1974	1973	1972	1971	1970	1969
After-tax Earnings (1969 = 100)	387	256	169	131	156	131	87	69	69	100
Capital Expenditures										
(a) Amount (1969 = 100)	412	304	216	169	206	141	92	91	155	100
(b) Percent of Internally Generated Funds	70	68	74	72	82	63	55	61	109	51
Debt-Equity Ratio (Corporate Limit: .40)	.24	.25	.31	.33	.19	.18	.21	.23	.24	.16
Timing of New Long-term Debt Issues				*					*	
Dividends per Share (1969 = 1)	1.37	1.22	1.14	1.13	1.05	1	1	1	1	1
Dividend Payout (Target Payout: .30-.40)	.28	.37	.35	.44	.34	.38	.56	.71	.71	.51

Table 6-1. (Continued)

Company B	1978	1977	1976	1975	1974	1973	1972	1971	1970	1969
After-tax Earnings (1969 = 100)	176	176	143	133	133	86	0	NEG	10	100
Capital Expenditures										
(a) Amount (1969 = 100)	158	167	98	220	150	101	64	64	128	100
(b) Percent of Internally Generated Funds	80	90	50	138	100	77	63	76	183	93
Debt-Equity Ratio (Corporate Limit: 1/1)	.51	.59	.67	.74	.57	.62	.72	.79	.85	.75
Timing of New Long-term Debt Issues				*					*	
Dividends per Share (1969 = 1)	1.74	1.44	1.15	.85	.73	.17	0	0	1	1
Dividend Payout (Target Payout: .25)	.25	.21	.20	.16	.14	.05	0	0	2.85	.25

during this period (see Table 6-2). Moreover, it chose to mark out long-term trends in the process rather than make short-term adjustments. Thus capital expenditures were substantially increased as a percentage of total allocations, while marketing expenditures gradually declined from 52 percent of the discretionary budget in 1969 to 45 percent in 1978. Not surprisingly, given the company's high-technology identity, research and development expenditures rose in an unbroken line from year to year; however, as a percentage of the total budget, R&D was held virtually constant throughout the decade.

A similar redistributive process is apparent in the record of management's allocations to individual product lines. Here again, most of the shifts reflected long-term commitments, such as the new emphasis on product line 2, evident in the 1973 allocations for marketing and capital expenditures, or the simultaneous falling-off in support for product line 1. However, the table reveals one-time events and short-term fluctuations as well: the 1974 surge in marketing expenditures for product line 4, for example, or the periodic shifts in capital expenditures for the same line. In summary, therefore, the company's record illustrates the process of resource reallocation which is an essential tool in management's overall funding strategy.

Competitive Strategy: The Level of Product-Market Support

The significance of the resource allocation process goes beyond its effect on a company's cash flow. These decisions are also a critical component in management's competitive strategy—the determination of who gets what in a world of limited strategic investment funds and competing product markets. For this reason allocations allow us to identify management's priorities at particular points in a company's history as well as relate those priorities to the financial goals system.

At company C, as previously noted, sales and earnings grew strongly and consistently over the ten-year period covered by the study. As Table 6-3 indicates, the company's activities were dominated by two product lines, while two others remained in an adolescent stage (with both recording strong growth and good returns). ROI was consistently strong among all four product lines.

Reviewing management's allocations among the product lines for three major discretionary expenditures (Table 6-2), it is clear that funds

Table 6-2. Company C: Index of Total Discretionary Expenditures (1969 = 100)

	Year by Year										Percentage of Total Outlay	
	1978	1977	1976	1975	1974	1973	1972	1971	1970	1969	1978	1969
Total Discretionary Expenditures												
Company	461	359	319	266	272	230	153	110	111	100	100	100
By Product Line												
1	39%	41%	40%	41%	41%	43%	51%	50%	51%	55%		
2	42	39	39	38	39	41	32	30	31	30		
3	10	10	11	11	10	9	10	9	8	7		
4	6	6	6	6	7	5	5	6	6	5		
Corporate and Other	3	4	4	4	3	2	2	5	4	3		
Marketing Expenditures												
Company	395	314	284	268	278	226	164	120	115	100	45	52
By Product Line												
1	41%	41%	39%	39%	34%	37%	50%	49%	50%	53%		
2	40	39	41	41	44	47	34	33	34	31		
3	12	13	13	13	11	11	11	12	9	9		
4	7	7	7	7	11	5	5	6	7	7		
R&D Expenditures												
Company	481	391	337	281	222	181	137	122	116	100	27	26
By Product Line												
1	36%	37%	38%	41%	45%	47%	48%	46%	46%	50%		
2	40	37	36	32	30	29	32	28	30	31		
3	7	8	6	7	7	7	7	5	5	3		
4	5	5	5	4	4	5	4	5	5	3		
Corporate and Other	12	13	15	16	14	12	9	6	14	13		
Capital Expenditures												
Company	592	430	381	241	318	296	144	70	99	100	28	22
By Product Line												
1	37%	43%	43%	47%	50%	51%	59%	63%	61%	63%		
2	47	42	41	36	36	36	28	27	27	26		
3	10	10	11	11	10	9	8	5	8	7		
4	6	5	5	6	4	4	5	5	4	4		

103

Table 6-3. Company C: Record of Product Line Performance

	Year by Year										Average Annual Growth Rate			Product Line (% of Total Sales)	
	1978	1977	1976	1975	1974	1973	1972	1971	1970	1969	Sales	O.P.	RONA	1978	1969
Company															
Index of Sales	514	405	336	292	263	197	142	112	108	100	18%			100	100
Index of Operating Profit (1969 = 100)	588	465	350	323	323	196	146	72	92	100		19%			
RONA	11%	10%	10%	11%	13%	9%	10%	8%	9%	11%			10%		
By Product Line															
1 Sales	310	247	212	188	168	154	131	123	109	100	12%			42	70
Operating Profit	416	316	253	226	205	142	121	105	95	100		15%			
RONA	18%	15%	14%	14%	13%	10%	11%	12%	11%	13%			13%		
2 Sales	1098	851	675	579	555	321	161	94	101	100	27%			43	20
Operating Profit	1100	900	600	620	780	400	220	20	100	100		27%			
RONA	10%	12%	9%	13%	18%	10%	11%	1%	7%	8%			10%		
3 Sales	815	660	590	485	385	285	205	155	120	100	23%			9	6
Operating Profit	1200	1000	1000	600	500	300	300	200	0	100		28%			
RONA	10%	11%	12%	8%	8%	6%	10%	10%	0	17%			9%		
4 Sales	754	577	446	400	300	208	161	123	115	100	22%			6	4
Operating Profit	700	600	300	400	100	100	100	100	100	100		22%			
RONA	10%	12%	8%	13%	4%	5%	6%	10%	13%	7%			8%		

flowed in response to need (growth) rather than superior ROI. Product line 1, the company's consistently superior rate of return performer, declined sharply from 70 percent of company sales in 1969 to 42 percent in 1978, despite the fact that it tripled its sales volume over the ten years. During the same period its share of discretionary resources fell as well: Overall, the line received only 39 percent of management's strategic investments in 1978 as compared to 54 percent in 1969. However, these allocations did not represent the neglect of profitability in favor of diversification, as might at first appear. On the contrary, they reflected management's recognition that its highly profitable primary business had matured, and that further market penetration was unlikely because of stiffening competition. With increasing limits on further investment in its most profitable area, therefore, management was diverting funds to develop alternative income streams. Even though these product lines fell short of the company's 18 percent RONA target, they were already recording healthy growth in profits. And at this stage at least, they provided the best prospect for the profitable employment of corporate resources in the future.

A similar process of corporate renewal and revitalization is evident in the allocations and performance data assembled for Company D (Tables 6-4 and 6-5). Here again, the record appears to show discretionary resources moving away from product lines producing the *highest* profit margins toward those with *lower* profit margins (including two which showed absolute losses for most of the period). Yet these allocations were financially rational, given an extended corporate time line and a healthy trust in the wisdom of management's new product line choices.

Because the company defines its corporate identity around consumer products in which strong brand franchises are the basis for market share and superior profit margins, "advertising, promotions, and special deals" is the discretionary expenditure with major long-term earnings potential. (Capital expenditures are secondary, as evidenced by the fact that the company has yet to develop a meaningful asset breakdown by product line.) As the tables indicate, the company's most profitable product lines received a declining share of this key expenditure over the ten-year period.[2] Product lines 1, 2, and 3 with average profit margins of 18 percent, 29 percent, and 20 percent respectively dropped from 62 percent in 1969 to 27 percent in 1978. In contrast, product line 8, which had an average operating margin of 14 percent, received a substantial increase from 25 percent to 50 percent, while the two loss lines (numbers 6 and 7) rose from 0 percent to 16 percent of total marketing expenditures.

Table 6-4. Company D: Index of Expenditures for Advertising, Promotions, and Special Deals (1969 = 100)

	Year by Year										Average Allocations by Product Line
	1969	1970	1971	1972	1973	1974	1975	1976	1977	1978	
Index of Total Outlays	100	110	119	145	191	188	159	185	213	243	
Allocations by Product Line											
1	33%	27%	25%	15%	22%	19%	12%	10%	8%	7%	18%
2	19	16	16	20	18	21	16	15	11	9	16
3	10	12	12	10	10	11	11	12	10	11	11
4	8	7	6	5	4	4	5	6	7	5	6
5	4	3	3	3	4	3	2	2	2	2	3
6	0	6	6	4	5	2	2	2	12	11	5
7	0	0	1	12	6	3	7	12	7	5	5
8	25	28	31	30	31	37	45	40	43	50	36

Given the fact that only product line 8 achieved the corporate target of 12 percent in sales and earnings, it would seem that management was chasing sales volume rather than superior profitability during this period. Apparently the allocations budget was geared to the relative growth rates of sales alone and not to current rates of return. Yet this explanation falls short of the truth. As Table 6-5 indicates, lines 1 and 2 were maturing product markets: Although still earning the highest rates of return, their sales had slowed or declined, competition had stiffened, and margins were gradually eroding. Corporate philosophy directed that new product markets be found, either internally or by acquisition, to sustain the company's long-term earnings capacity and employ corporate resources. Further, management knew that it would take five to ten years for some of these new product markets to develop a meaningful brand franchise and defensible market share, or even to turn a profit. In the interim, therefore, corporate resources were being diverted year after year from old, relatively high-return product lines, incapable of absorbing more resources, to new no-return or low-return product lines with long-term earnings potential. Clearly management hoped that over time these products would generate the earning power which lines 1 and 2 had produced for several decades and were only now losing.

A different picture emerges from the allocations and performance records of Company E, a more widely diversified and capital-intensive company (Tables 6-6 and 6-7). Product line 3 was this company's clear winner in growth and in return (both average and trend). Consistent with this performance, the line received a rising share of the capital budget (as high as 26 percent in recent years). Conversely, management withheld capital funds from product line 6, which had experienced actual losses in eight of the past eleven years and had shown a negative growth rate of sales. Although the line was still in existence in 1979—and had even registered a dramatic, but presumably temporary, improvement in ROI—it is evident that its funding had been cut off as of 1975. Thus clear winners and losers were given their appropriate rewards by this management.

However, Company E's management also made funding decisions in which there was less apparent correlation between performance and reward. Product line 1, for example, received the lion's share of the company's capital expenditures (some 24 percent on average), while simultaneously turning in consistently poor ROI performances. (The line ranked fourth of six on average and fell to last place in 1978–79.) In this case it seems reasonable to conclude that the managers' sustained commitment

Table 6-5. Company D: Record of Product Line Performance

	Year by Year										Average Annual			Product Line (% of Total Sales)	
											Growth Rate		O.P. as % of Sales		
	1978	1977	1976	1975	1974	1973	1972	1971	1970	1969	Sales	O.P.		1978	1969
Company															
Index of Sales	336	281	253	215	195	170	144	122	110	100	13%				
Index of Operating Profit (1969 = 100)	217	179	162	111	133	106	114	106	100	100		8%			
O.P. as % of Sales	22%	14%	14%	17%	15%	14%	17%	19%	19%	22%			17		
By Product Line															
1 Sales	89	90	91	89	96	103	88	99	100	100	(1)			6	23
Operating Profit	129	118	98	76	59	51	101	90	80	100		3			
O.P. as % of Sales	27%	24%	20%	16%	12%	9%	21%	17%	15%	19%			18		
2 Sales	148	148	149	129	147	151	143	116	108	100	4			7	17
Operating Profit	125	115	103	88	121	138	149	130	114	100		2			
O.P. as % of Sales	28%	25%	23%	22%	27%	30%	34%	37%	34%	33%			29		

#		C1	C2	C3	C4	C5	C6	C7	C8	C9	C10	C11	C12	C13	C14	C15
3	Sales	267	226	230	172	159	143	129	118	116	100	10	8	20	10	13
	Operating Profit	211	164	168	107	101	88	98	97	105	100					
	O.P. as % of Sales	20%	20%	19%	16%	16%	16%	20%	21%	23%	26%					
4	Sales	222	237	218	138	91	95	94	92	94	100	8	(17)	7	4	6
	Operating Profit	14	114	33	NEG	76	62	57	48	76	100					
	O.P. as % of Sales	1%	6%	2%	6%	10%	8%	8%	6%	10%	12%					
5	Sales	200	151	133	142	158	153	110	110	102	100	7	14	6	1	2
	Operating Profit	366	366	66	66	400	66	133	133	133	100					
	O.P. as % of Sales	9%	12%	3%	2%	13%	2%	6%	6%	7%	5%					
6	Sales	1900	1000	348	272	308	344	296	244	100	0	39	—	(68)	5	0
	Operating Profit	100	NEG	NEG	NEG	NEG	NEG	NEG	NEG	NEG	NEG					
	O.P. as % of Sales	6%	(32%)	(14%)	(27%)	(21%)	(67%)	(10%)	(28%)	(84%)	(400%)					
7	Sales	204	213	198	111	78	113	100	NEG			13	—	(22)	3	0
	Operating Profit	73	100	NEG	NEG	NEG	NEG	NEG	(151%)							
	O.P. as % of Sales	5%	6%	(14%)	(18%)	(8%)	(9%)	(32%)								
8	Sales	485	386	337	310	273	210	166	137	117	100	17	13	14	50	34
	Operating Profit	349	260	248	198	217	159	134	113	102	100					
	O.P. as % of Sales	13%	12%	13%	12%	14%	14%	15%	15%	16%	18%					

Table 6-6. Company E: Index of Capital Expenditures (1969 = 100)

	Year by Year											Average Allocations by Product Line
	1979	1978	1977	1976	1975	1974	1973	1972	1971	1970	1969	
Index of Total Outlays	134	158	167	98	220	150	101	64	64	128	100	
Allocations by Product Line												
1	31%	28%	32%	27%	42%	13%	13%	12%	15%	NA	NA	24%
2	25	22	16	26	5	9	38	28	10	NA	NA	20
3	13	21	26	20	7	22	9	4	7	NA	NA	14
4	10	9	14	6	3	7	11	12	28	NA	NA	11
5	18	19	9	13	13	17	9	11	18	NA	NA	14
6	0	0	2	6	29	31	19	32	22	NA	NA	16
Other	3	1	1	2	1	1	1	1	0	NA	NA	1

to the line was related to its relatively high growth rate of sales and not to its growth in profits or ROI to date.

The need to sustain existing market positions also appears to have been influential in other funding decisions at Company E. Of the company's remaining lines, only number 4 succeeded in meeting RONA and earnings growth rate objectives. (Indeed, management had recently lowered the latter from 15 percent to 10 percent in recognition of that fact.) Yet the managers continued to deploy available capital resources among the various lines with a relatively even hand, as Table 6-6 indicates. Thus the picture which emerges from these data suggests that management was prepared to nurse along a portfolio with very mixed performance—for the time being, at least.[3]

Business Strategy: The Choice of Product Markets

The third—and most important—issue latent in the resource allocation process is management's business strategy, the selection of the product markets in which the company will compete. Complex in their own right, these portfolio choices are further complicated by the realities that characterize the product-market investments of large, relatively mature industrial enterprises. As has been noted, the income streams of such firms are normally dominated by a few long-term, large market-share product-market positions which have taken decades to develop. Because of economic and psychological factors, these positions are as difficult to abandon as they are to initiate. Thus meaningful strategic investment choices are apt to be made in response to occasional, somewhat random windows of opportunity rather than to occur in a continuous stream.

As part of this study the participating managements were asked to identify key strategic product-market decisions made in their companies during the past ten years. By definition, therefore, these were investment decisions in which top management took personal control of the decision process. Their choices (approximately two dozen in all) fell into four broad categories. These were: the decision to undertake a major plant modernization or expansion of capacity in an existing product line; the decision to disinvest in or divest an established product line; the decision to develop a major new product line through internal research and development; and the decision to add to a new product line through the acquisition of an existing independent enterprise.[4]

Table 6-7. Company E: Record of Product Line Performance

| | Year by Year | | | | | | | | | | | Average Annual | | O.P. | Product Line (% of Total Sales) | |
| | | | | | | | | | | | | Growth Rate | | as % of | | |
	1979	1978	1977	1976	1975	1974	1973	1972	1971	1970	1969	Sales	O.P.	Sales	1979	1969
Company																
Index of Sales	217	187	170	165	159	149	121	114	108	106	100	7%				
Index of Operating Profit (1969 = 100)	226	146	180	148	124	126	90	62	58	44	100		8%	6%		
RONA	9%	9%	8%	7%	8%	8%	6%	2%	2%	3%	7%					
By Product Line																
1 Sales	295	255	239	208	163	156	139	113	101	103	100	10%			12	9
Operating Profit	106	22	145	122	112	133	73	40	44	71	100		1%	9%		
RONA	5%	1%	8%	8%	10%	17%	9%	6%	6%	11%	18%					

Group	Measure															
2	Sales	254	228	217	206	189	177	147	130	118	113	100		16	23
	Operating Profit (1971 = 100)	81	70	51	75	76	61	19	51	100	—	—			
	RONA	16%	15%	14%	12%	9%	15%	14%	16%	13%	—	—	9%	(3%)	14%
3	Sales	318	240	219	210	215	183	134	112	112	115	100		14	9
	Operating Profit	1333	796	941	1050	1733	1062	350	196	175	158	100			
	RONA	27%	21%	29%	38%	69%	48%	21%	13%	9%	7%	5%	11%	27%	26%
4	Sales	263	229	205	188	202	170	127	124	120	108	100		25	22
	Operating Profit	173	131	224	187	88	30	19	NEG	76	104	100			
	RONA	10%	9%	16%	15%	7%	2%	2%	(2%)	8%	13%	14%	9%	5%	8%
5	Sales	191	162	136	128	108	121	108	108	100	102	100		18	21
	Operating Profit	170	169	143	105	56	120	115	86	61	60	100			
	RONA	15%	18%	17%	13%	8%	17%	17%	13%	8%	7%	14%	6%	5%	13%
6	Sales	51	51	53	91	104	107	90	94	96	97	100		4	14
	Operating Profit	160	93	NEG	NEG	NEG	NEG	NEG	NEG	NEG	NEG	100			
	RONA	55%	42%	(11%)	(18%)	(22%)	(22%)	(6%)	(3%)	(3%)	(3%)	5%	6%	4%	NEG

Predictably, there were various precipitating incidents for these decisions including one-time opportunities, competitors' actions, internal circumstances, and arbitrary choices made by strong corporate leaders. However, interviews and document searches indicated that the decision process was similar from company to company and case to case. Invariably, a great deal was at stake, and strong voices were heard on both sides. The issues were complex, the evidence hard to read, the relevant considerations subjective as well as objective. Thus it is not surprising that clear cause-and-effect relationships were hard to trace—even when reason predominated in the decision-making process.

*Case One   A Proposal For a $100 Million-plus
Renovation of an Aging Plant*

This management had postponed modernization at one of its major plants for a number of years because of limited corporate discretionary funds. However, the plant was clearly operating at a cost disadvantage, and a decision to shut down, renovate, or rebuild could no longer be avoided. Eventually a final recommendation would have to be made to the board of directors. In the meantime management debated its options, drawing on personal experience as well as two detailed analytical studies prepared as part of the review process.

The debate was focused on the specific plant and the particular expenditures required for each of the options. (These ranged from $30 million for shutting down the plant to $200 million for a complete rebuilding.) However, in hindsight it was clear that the real issue was the future of the entire traditional product line—the historical backbone which represented over one-third of the company's total earning power. In recent years this product line had demonstrated only sluggish growth and modest returns on investment. Yet entry into the industry was difficult, because of its capital-intensive nature, and there were also formidable economic, human, and psychological barriers to exit. Consequently any decision that called into question the viability of the entire product line was taken very seriously.

Throughout the decision-making process growth was a prominent topic and a fundamental source of conflict. Several executives worried about the effect of the industry's weak growth on the organization. As one observed, "The important thing about growth beyond just financial consideration is that that's how you get the best people. It's more exciting for an organization. The purpose of our business is to create value . . . for *all* stakeholders, including the shareholders." For him the message was clear: ROI attracts capital, but growth attracts people (that is, superior management). Given a compound growth rate of only 3 percent, "there was talk up and down the hall that we ought to get out of the business."

Additionally, opinion was divided from the start over the advantages of growth from within versus growth by acquisition. The company had pursued both options, and each strategy had its spokesmen, although some who favored acquisition felt that it was not considered seriously enough. As one interviewee commented, "Internal management really doesn't want acquisitions. There is nothing in it for them. All they get is newcomers who will compete with them [for resources]." From this perspective, therefore, management's eventual decision to recommit reflected its bias toward the familiar. Modest but assured and personally rewarding growth was preferable to the more exciting growth available in a competing division.

This analysis omits the most important considerations in the managers' thinking, however. Chief among them was their fear of the adverse consequences that would be created by closing the plant. Such a decision would send a strong signal to competitors, investors, and employees at a time when the competition was "going all out," and it was difficult to see what would be gained in return (even if some executives believed that "people who should get out won't"). In the short term the most visible effect of a closing would be a substantial write-off of book value with a serious one-time impact on earnings per share. Longer term, the absence of a viable alternative to this major segment of the corporate earnings base suggested that there would be an extended, costly, and uncertain period associated with "giving up" on the industry with which the firm's name was most closely associated.

Under the circumstances management responded by seeking to delay and minimize the investment necessary to sustain the company's competitive position. The financial goals system reinforced this decision in several regards. Most obvious, perhaps, was the fact that the planned expenditures were temporarily forced down from $200 million to $90 million by the limits of self-sustaining growth and the vigorous competition for funds within the corporate capital market. (That management would have to come back in for more money at a later date was apparent to all. As one board member knowingly commented when faced with this request, "You'll be back, it's only a question of when.") In addition, the goals system established the terms in which management and the board thought about the company's growth and returns.

Because the corporate self-sustaining RONA of 12 percent was obviously unattainable under any analysis based on reasonable assumptions, it is particularly interesting to follow management's logic on the subject of the plant's anticipated return. As a first step the goal was shifted to 9 percent, a figure judged attainable on the basis of industry performance, and one which could fund growth of 4-1/2 percent in conjunction with the firm's other goals. However, even this return appeared to be an unlikely prospect for the immediate future. Consequently, when the board finally approved management's proposal, it did so with the clear understanding that the plant would achieve the desired 9 percent RONA *within five years.* The board took this obligation seriously, as did the managers, one of whom commented: "We've sweated that out. The Board has that commitment in its pocket and pulls it out yearly." Clearly both groups were concerned that the plant become self-funding—and even yield a small surplus—as quickly as possible.

*Case Two   Divestiture of an Established
Product Market*

Divestiture was an attractive alternative for the management of this company. The division in question manufactured and sold an industrial product, whereas the company was primarily engaged in consumer goods. Thus the division failed to mesh with either the company's dominant product-market thrust or its philosophy, which emphasized the value of a distinctive product-market identity. Persuaded that a consistent identity served to increase internal commitment and expertise, while also enhancing the company's external reputation and image, management rejected the "conglomerate" approach that the industrial division's presence seemed to require.

Economic factors also worked against the division's tenure. The industry was cyclical, its growth and ROI potential were inferior, and it was capital intensive. In addition, the company's present position in the industry demanded that it "grow or get out." But growth would require a major capital expenditure which management was reluctant to undertake, because it would severely constrain the funding for the company's primary market positions.

In this context it proved easy to revive a decision made nearly ten years earlier. At that time the company's top management had tried to sell the industrial division, but it had been unable to get a satisfactory price. Consequently, the division had been withdrawn from the market, to be built up in anticipation of a sale at some later appropriate time. Interest in a sale had ebbed and flowed during the interim, as the division's year-to-year performance followed its cyclical course. However, for most of this period the company was led by a chief executive who "hated to get out of anything." Thus divestiture did not become a serious option again until the company's leadership changed. Not surprisingly, the advent of new men was the trigger for action. The division was sold as an operating entity, at a price that exceeded book value and provided a net after-tax gain. Because management had always been "uncomfortable" with the division, it was convinced that "the employees [would] be better understood and better off with the new management." Also, management was pleased that funds freed up by the sale could be used to support aggressive growth goals in other divisions—a spur to divestiture from the start.

Case Three   Investments in New Product Development

In 1974–75 the management of this high-technology company faced a choice between two new product opportunities developed by its research and development staff. Although the company would be viewed as one of the strongest in the country by most people, it was experiencing a period of financial stress. An overall capital budget had been worked out which would maintain the company's conservative debt-to-capitalization ratio by relying on internally generated funds and their increment of debt only. But the budget had a real price in terms of forgone opportunities. As one executive commented at the time, the figure "was initially designed to maintain a 30 percent ratio, is now forecast to maintain it at 33 percent, [and] a lower forecast of earnings would produce 37 percent. This budget is attained only at the cost of the cancellation or deferral of very attractive projects."

In choosing to safeguard its highly conservative debt-equity ratio, management was thinking about more than tradition. With the future of the company bound up in a strong market-leadership role in internally developed, technology-based product innovations, the ability to borrow at will was a vital asset. New developments could occur unexpectedly, and the company had to be in a position to move quickly: "If we make a breakthrough, we don't want to be at the 40 percent debt level. We need the flexibility (and the certainty) to move on it if we get a break. Flexibility for the future is needed more than safety. . . . We can't risk the corporation in favor of a little better performance. Our first priority is survival."

Management was equally unwilling to increase the capital budget by reducing dividends. In an internal memorandum entitled, "Capability to Finance Capital Authorization Program," the direct tradeoff between dividends per share and the level of required borrowing was noted. But both the financial office and the planning group assumed that per share dividends would continue to be "reasonably in line" with projected earnings (although they also expected that the payout would gradually decline over time as earnings improved). Thus, in the terms of this study, the budget was worked out in express recognition of the need to balance the self-sustaining growth equation without violating targeted debt or dividend payout objectives.

In this atmosphere, with the company's needs pressing on the limits of the internal capital market, the budget was designed to state corporate priorities clearly. Projects were first segmented into three categories: "(1) nondiscretionary projects (e.g., projects underway, legal requirements); (2) projects vital to the better performance of product lines; and (3) [projects] difficult to forego but basically discretionary." Those in the first two groups received the go-ahead, while those in the third were further subdivided into: "(a) backward integration projects; (b) projects having clear long-term interest but timing subject to . . . an acceptable financial position; and (c) potentially attractive projects with continuing areas of uncertainty." These projects—at the margin because they were not central to the established product-market mainstream, or could be deferred without seriously damaging their potential, or had above-average payoff uncertainties—had to compete for the capital budget's remaining available funds. When hard choices had to be made, they were the most vulnerable to being cut.

Both the competing projects fell into the third category. Project A called for the construction of a plant to process one of the company's raw materials. The plant had been requested by a substantial end-user, and the project offered a guaranteed return on investment of 17 percent–19 percent. In management's own words, "This project was a clear winner financially speaking. At any other time we would have done it. But the problem was that we didn't *have* to do it, and since we were in the process of cutting everyone to the bone, we decided not to do something we didn't absolutely have to." In a world of capital scarcity even a high and riskless return was not enough. This was the "easy" decision from management's perspective.

Its competitor, Project B, provided no such easy answer. This project represented an investment in a potentially new and exciting family of products. But the estimated return on investment was 15 percent (less than Project A's), and there was unusual uncertainty about the amount and timing of returns. As one executive commented, "This was one where a rational man might stop." Nevertheless, the company did not stop. Management deferred immediate action but provided enough funding to keep the project alive. In explanation the same executive went on to add, "We're a technology-based company and we have few breakthroughs. This was potentially a whole new field and we felt it ought to be *ours*. . . . Things get a little irrational at times. . . ."

On balance, this executive's confession of irrationality may well have been misplaced. Examined carefully, these decisions are clearly consistent with the priorities established by the overall capital budget. Sustaining major, mainstream product-market positions came first on top management's list. Consequently, Project B deserved to get the go-ahead, because it had the potential to become the corporate mainstream's next generation. Its long-term sustained payoff was preferable to the discounted values of measurable near-term cash flow or net-income impact, however riskless, provided by Project A.

The fact that specific growth or rate of return targets played little, if any, direct part in these decisions is also noteworthy. Management's broad and generalized perceptions of the product-market opportunities related to traditional corporate strengths were more significant by far. As one top manager observed, while reflecting on the company's organization:

> We don't want to force arbitrariness from the top. You can't be run by the numbers in a multi-product company. When you establish a threshold rate of return a lot of good projects will go down the drain . . . . [The CEO of ITT] runs it like a banker because it's a true conglomerate. . . . We don't operate that way. We have a much more cohesive culture. . . . We support our weaknesses from within . . . moreover I think [our system] has the potential for being tougher . . . because it recognizes human nature. I think the trend of business is away from the detached quantitative evaluations and towards a more personal type of management.

Many of this executive's peers in the other companies shared his doubts about the wisdom of making strategic product-market decisions on the basis of numbers alone. Discounted cash flow analytical methods were used by all the companies in the study. But the results were subject to considerable qualification by top managements as they made their investment choices.

The Role of Traditional Investment Analysis in Strategic Decision Making

Discounted cash flow analysis of individual investment projects is strongly endorsed by academics and widely accepted in the business community. Every company included in this study had a financial staff properly trained and experienced in DCF analysis. All were in full command of its methodology, and all applied the analysis appropriately and consistently to their annual capital budget reviews.

Moreover, modern DCF analysis captures the key elements of sound economic and financial reasoning with respect to maximizing the financial benefit from investment on an incremental, project-by-project decision basis. Barring some deliberate distortion, all available data on the anticipated net cash-flow consequences of an investment decision are objectively arrayed over the project's economic life and systematically ranked. These rankings (given in terms of the project's net present value or internal rate of return) are determined by reference to the risk-adjusted hurdle rate that reflects the corporation's minimum acceptable return—a rate usually described as its cost of capital. Thus the analysis produces a list of investment proposals that equal or exceed the investment hurdle rate and promise the maximum financial benefit. Emotion, self-interest, ego, and rules of thumb are appropriately excluded from this economically rational analysis. Its relevance for the resource-allocation process is difficult to dispute.

Nevertheless, despite its universal availability and practical appeal, formal DCF analysis was at best only a partial discipline in the actual resource allocation process. In practice it did not provide the integrating framework within which the long-term strategic distribution of discretionary resources among competing product lines took place. As executives from several companies indicated, DCF analyses were subject to a range of qualifications in the formal decision process:

> Viable plans determine money [made available]. Strategy and market positions are the important part of any plan, not ROI.

The twenty businesses are classified into six [strategic] categories indicating declining priority, from "superthrust" at the top to "sustain" and "selective" at the bottom. Classifications are established by top management, though appeal can be made by division managers. Allocations are made starting with superthrust category businesses and working down the hierarchy. Top management decides on the overall level of expenditure. "Baseline spending" for maintenance and cost reduction (about 30% of the total capital budget) are decided by strategic-category percentage guidelines and are "owned" by the divisions.

The Company has no formal investment hurdle rates. We know what our cost of capital is . . . but we don't want to use it as a hurdle rate. For example, on energy savings, it may look like an 8% return now, but it may turn out to be 20% later. All our hurdle rates inevitably lead to fudging the numbers. . . . [Our Company] argues, "If it makes good business sense, do it." DCF is too short term for strategy. . . . On the other [hand], you can't ignore it.

Every five years you have one [major] decision and then you have four years of commitment. On *that* decision an Internal Rate of Return analysis is run to see if it makes any sense at all, but that isn't the determining factor. [Industry] decisions dominate years of spending. We've decided that we're in this industry to stay and it's full speed ahead and damn the torpedoes.

Capital budgeting at [name of company] is heavily dominated by a strategic matrix framework. Rate of growth and share of market for each business seem to be the key elements determining the resources to be allocated. Little or no mention of conventional capital budgeting criteria can be found. Hurdle rates are not often used around here. We've gotten away from a "project mentality."

The financial policies and procedures manual does not provide hurdle rates. After submitting incremental analysis, requests . . . are forwarded to the corporate controller who reviews them and comments on their linkages to strategy and performance in the given product area. Finally, the capital budgets for the whole company are combined to determine if the level of spending agrees with the cash generation plan and the overall corporate strategy.

Like many of those quoted above, the managers at one of the consumer products companies carried out a very sophisticated and detailed DCF process in reviewing investment proposals. Yet this elaborate set of economic considerations seemed almost to exist outside the final decision-making process. As one of the divisional managers noted in discussing a particular product-market decision, "ROI is a hurdle that you must explain, but it certainly isn't the whole picture. Recently a competitor introduced a new product. It isn't going to make it [financially], but we have to have the product for defensive reasons."

Comments by other executives indicated that this decision accurately reflected top management's approach to strategic investments. For many this was all to the good. As the vice-president for product planning noted approvingly, "Something we don't have now, and the chief financial officer has resisted, is a formal hurdle rate. We have a target, but lots of investments get made at less than the target." However, others were less enthusiastic, among them this manager who commented, "ROI is just not used that much around here. Maybe top management doesn't understand it or maybe they are just gut managers."

The evidence that a substantial amount of capital expenditure bypasses the formal review process could be dismissed by following the lead of the last interviewee and attributing it to ignorance or gut feeling. Certainly intuition, preconception, opinion, and self-interest play an important role in real-world investment decisions just as they do in other areas of human activity. However, careful consideration suggests that there are substantive, rational reasons for the modest role given to DCF analysis by top management in the decision-making process. Comparing the underlying assumptions of project analysis with the underlying philosophy of strategic choice described here, we find two different sets of financial assumptions. Both are logical and internally consistent, but one works from without, while the other works from within.

Formal DCF analysis is premised on the following assumptions:

- The sole purpose of corporate investment is to increase shareholder wealth.

- A certain amount of wealth available in the near future is always preferable to the same amount of wealth in the longer term.

- Corporate wealth should be increased only if the increase equals or exceeds that which an equity investor could earn elsewhere in the industry or in the economy for comparable risk.

- The context for assessing comparable risk consists of any and all investment opportunities that have financial characteristics compatible with the goals of objective, disinterested, diversified public investors. Any proposal that does not meet this standard should be denied investment funds.

- Funds are always available in unlimited amounts for any investment that meets or exceeds the market rate of return.

In contrast, management considers strategic investment choices in a framework defined by these assumptions:

- The increase of shareholder wealth is only one of a number of corporate purposes arrived at in response to the various constituent groups on whom the company's long-term survival and well-being depend. Product-market choices are equally (or more) important, because they support the unbroken succession of carefully selected positions which sustain major segments of corporate overhead over extended periods of time.

- Although a dollar today is generally more beneficial and more certain than a dollar tomorrow, single present-value or rate of return calculations obscure critical cash flow time profiles. As has been seen, management gives the highest priority to maintaining the continuity of the month-to-month and year-to-year aggregate cash inflows available to meet foreseen and unforeseen strategic needs as they arise. In this context it is the anticipated performance of the entire income stream which dominates the investment decision and not the marginal return on an increment of investment related to the stream. And this logic—as much as anything—explains the apparent rejection of ROI data as the key consideration in determining investment projects. Intent on developing the future income streams that will contribute to corporate survival, management is prepared to sacrifice some degree of near-term return for long-term benefits.

- Corporate wealth should be increased whenever the increase will enhance the company's survival and opportunity potential. Therefore, the most meaningful investment alternatives are those provided by product-market income streams compatible with the company's perceived competence and competitive advantage. Similarly, the real opportunity cost of an investment decision is defined by the viable *corporate* alternatives that have been foregone.

- The context for assessing investment risks is defined by internal factors: the opportunities available to this particular enterprise and appropriate to its business mission. Thus, the best portfolio is a limited number of long-term, strong, and successful competitive positions in product markets compatible with perceived corporate strengths. Given management's commitment to succeed in all such initiatives, the question is not whether funds should be invested, but how they should be allocated.

- Strategic discretionary resources are finite, because funds are not always available from the public capital market in the right amount, at the right time, on acceptable terms. In assessing the benefits of vital strategic investments, therefore, immediate financial returns take second place to the spectrum of goals associated with the company's defined business mission and its long-term well-being.

The fundamental differences among these sets of assumptions do not consign DCF analysis to oblivion. On the contrary, it fills several critical functions. Most obvious, perhaps, is the fact that proposals must be well thought out and viable to survive the analytical process. Thus DCF provides an extremely useful framework for processing individual investment decisions, as the companies' actual practice attests. In addition, DCF analysis provides essential current information for tracking investments in established product markets once decisions have been made. Should there be persistent evidence that returns are significantly above or below management's original expectations, the level of resources committed to the particular income stream can be modified accordingly. Finally, analytical methods are increasingly reflective of strategic investment realities. Thus, as methods are further refined, they are likely to lend themselves to the strategic forest as well as to individual investment trees.[5]

Nevertheless, the grounds for a persistent conflict between management's strategic-investment choices and those supported by market-defined investment criteria continue to exist. Responsive to multiple goals and multiple constituencies, professional managers differ significantly from those who think only in terms of diversified public investors and capital-market alternatives in ranking investment options.

The Logic of Strategic Investment Choices

The managers of these companies classified particular investment choices as "strategic" for several reasons. Foremost among them was the fact that each of the designated proposals presented management with an opportunity to initiate, stimulate, or abort an investment revenue chain of major importance to the company's total performance. Indeed, the specific investment characteristics of the proposal were secondary to the product-market income stream of which it was a part. Hence it is not surprising that management's attention was focused on the entire stream and not on the individual proposal, as the benefits to be derived from this potential or actual component of the corporate portfolio were evaluated.

In determining whether an investment was the right choice, the first question to be answered was that of fit: Was the proposal compatible with the company's established business mission, perceived organizational strengths, and managerial preferences? Often the managers could not define fit, except in the broadest terms; but, like good art, they knew it when they saw it. Thus this question had to elicit the conviction that *this* company and this management could meet or exceed competitive standards of productivity and profitability on a *sustained basis*. Financial performance alone did not suffice when resources were scarce.

A second question dealt with the relationship between the company's existing financial goals and the proposal's expected performance. (Here again, it is important to emphasize that the performance in question was not primarily—or even importantly—the financial profile of the specific investment project but, rather, the product-market income stream of which it was a part. To the extent that the project returns were influential, it was because they were assumed to be representative of the broader family of investments to come.) Top managers' performance expectations were based on information drawn from their own experience and that of their competitors, and they were not precise. Nevertheless, they produced an expected-performance ranking among the viable product-market options which had a powerful influence on the allocation of resources.

As this last observation indicates, the financial goals system did not usually generate specific decision rules for individual investment choices. Instead it created the context, or general financial environment, within which tradeoffs were decided. For example, top managers clearly favored income streams that promised a relatively high return on investment, especially when the returns were stable over time and management was confident of its organization's ability to deliver. (Once again, the question of fit arises.) At the same time, issues of scale and growth complicated their investment choices.

Unless high prospective returns were associated with the potential for growth and for a scale of operations capable of supporting the organization over an extended period of time, they paled beside management's persistent concern for organizational survival. In other words, *both* growth and ROI were essential. And yet, inevitably, growth and high rates of return were not concurrent characteristics of product-market development, particularly in capital-intensive industries. Growth (especially growth in investment) tends to precede superior profits, often by a long interval. Hence the classic management tradeoff arises: which should dominate—growth or ROI?

This question poses no problem for a management with access to infinite supplies of capital and managerial talent. But the capital market described here—the capital market defined by these managers—was distinctly finite, and funding choices were a vital issue. Faced with the necessity of balancing funds flows month by month and quarter by quarter, these managements had to juggle their priorities, as their choices demonstrate. Cash-deficit income streams with high potential returns had to be weighted against low-return, cash-surplus income streams. Future profitability (and future solvency) had to be balanced against current profitability and the current solvency which ensured that there would be a future.

The need to fund both immediate and future priorities could also precipitate a test of management's convictions about its debt and dividend policies, if retained earnings and new debt were insufficient to supply all the requisite funds. Individual managements' solutions to this situation differed, as we have seen. But they tended to share an instinctive response when matters of strategic importance were at stake: Spend only what is necessary to keep the best options open. In one case this meant preserving a cash cow; in another, keeping a promising calf alive. In both the pacing of strategic investments to match the flow of funds from plannable sources presented a difficult test of priorities between short-term sufficiency and long-term competitive survival.

To these key considerations of fit, financial promise, and funding, a fourth must be added: the information the decision conveys—positive or negative—to insiders and outsiders about the company's strategic direction and management's commitment to make it work. This was a major issue in each of the strategic business decisions we have examined, particularly the first. Management has to anticipate its message; and it must also anticipate the response that message will evoke from employees, customers, and competitors, the key corporate constituents for whom continuity is critical. Indeed, a decision's value as a signal often dominates—or even overrides—the immediate value of the investment, because of the inescapable interdependence among the enterprise and its several constituencies.

Notes

1. Management's commitment to self-sustaining growth in established product markets also accounts for the persistence—and importance—of this ongoing debate. As we have seen, there was little room for slack in the financial goals systems of the companies studied. Management did not plan to issue new equity to fund established product markets. Existing financial reserves were not available for *planned* expenditures. Existing assets were used efficiently so that the sales-to-assets ratio approached the highest possible level. Thus all the goals were in direct contention and had to be reconciled, or the system would be thrown out of balance.

2. We assume, as the company does, that there is a rough correlation between operating margins and ROI.

3. Because of the spasmodic character of capital expenditures, it is difficult to use them to document strategy, even over a ten-year period.

4. Acquisitions are discussed in Chapter 8.

5. Walter Carl Kester, "Growth Options and Investment: A Dynamic Perspective on the Firm's Allocation of Resources" (Ph.D. dissertation, Harvard University, 1981); Stewart C. Meyers, "Finance Theory and Financial Strategy," *Interfaces*, in press; J. E. Broyles and J. A. Cooper, "Growth Opportunities and Real Investment Decisions" in *Risk, Capital Costs, and Project Financing Decisions*, ed. Frans G. J. Derkinderen and Roy L. Crum (The Hague: Nijhoff Publishing, 1981), pp. 107–18.

7

Performance Against Plan: Short-term Management and the Goals System

The effects of a formal goals system are far reaching. Top management's financial goals discipline the performance of the corporation as a whole and as a set of discrete product markets or strategic business units. In addition, these goals are reinforced by executive compensation plans, which are designed to reward individual managers for their contributions to the growth of corporate wealth. Yet corporate managers have surprisingly little freedom to alter these goals in the three- to five-year period covered by most financial plans. On the contrary, in the short run their choices are constrained and circumscribed by forces beyond their immediate control, because they reflect commitments to existing constituencies and operating realities created by past decisions and economic events. Only in the longer run can management successfully modify its environment to achieve goals and strategies of its own choosing.

The Discipline of the Goals System

This study indicates clearly the disciplinary power of the goals system on corporate financial objectives. During the period under review, managements were consciously aiming for greater self-sufficiency and self-sustaining growth. At the same time they were adjusting these goals to the realities of corporate performance. Thus there was a discernible relation between performance and plan, although the two were rarely, if ever, perfectly aligned.

Figure 7-1 illustrates this relationship by tracking one company's performance against the set of specific numerical targets its management had chosen for the rate of growth, RONA, and debt-equity ratio. At any given time this set can be represented by a point on the graph (T_1 and, later, T_2).[1] As the figure indicates, company A's management modified both sets of criteria during the eleven-year period plotted on the graph. The targets for growth and RONA were revised upward, while the self-

Figure 7:1   Company A: Record of Performance, 1968-78

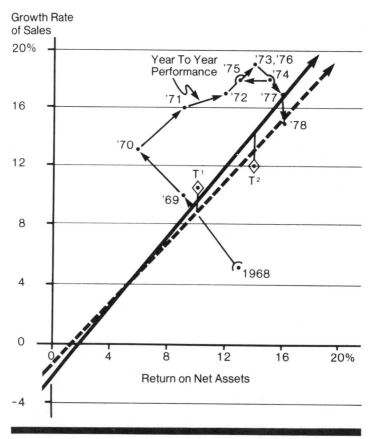

T¹ = Original Targets for Growth and RONA
T² = Current Targets for Growth and RONA
Broken Line = Path of Self-Sustaining Growth with Original Goals (T¹)
Solid Line = Path of Self-Sustaining Growth with Current Goals (T²)

sustaining growth line was also tilted modestly upward through revisions in the company's targeted payout and debt-equity ratio. (Here, as elsewhere in this chapter, the dates for major revisions in goals have been omitted to preclude company identification.) Both changes reflected the discipline of the goals system.

In 1968 the company had a growth rate that was below target and a return on net assets that was above target, a combination consistent with the generation of surplus investment funds. Management's aggressive growth and diversification strategies quickly brought the company's sluggish growth up to target and beyond; but the consequences for the company's returns and funds flows were considerable. As can be seen, the company did not achieve its RONA objective again until 1973. As serious, if not more so, were its nine years of above-the-line performance, that is, performance in the sector implying substantial funds-flow deficits. Apparently management had been so carried away by opportunity and events that it had gone beyond a financially prudent level of growth.

Given what has been said about the goals system's discipline and the need for balanced funds flows, how was this growth sustained? The most obvious explanation would seem to be that the company had a war chest of unused funds available during these years of rapid expansion. But in fact management had neither liquid assets nor idle debt capacity to call on. A dramatic improvement in asset turnover, which nearly doubled during the eleven years, provided some of the requisite funds, and others were supplied by a modest decline in the dividend payout. However, the most significant assistance came from new equity, issued in exchange for the assets and earnings of new subsidiaries. In other words, management was not pursuing a strategy of self-sufficiency during these years, because of its desire to replace mature product markets with new ones promising higher rates of growth and return on investment.[2]

Yet even under these circumstances, the effects of funds-flow pressure can be seen in the company's changing goals. The impact on the corporate targets for growth and RONA is most obvious. These targets shifted from a modest deficit (planned or unplanned) at the beginning of the period to a surplus deliberately planned to generate reserves. Strict internal consistency would, of course, dictate a slightly lower RONA target or a slightly higher growth rate. But in this case it seems likely that management was trying to accumulate funds as a defensive or offensive weapon after its expansionary phase.

Management's decision to revise its debt and dividend policies was similarly linked to the company's need for funds. As can be seen, leverage was modestly increased at the same time that the company's overall borrowing capacity rose because of the new equity issues. In fact, by the end of the period the debt-equity ratio was significantly below target, thereby providing an additional reserve to complement the surplus funds management had targeted.

Corporate performance was likewise being disciplined by the goals system during this period. As Figure 7-1 makes plain, the company's track record moved in a clockwise fashion toward self-sufficiency. The substantial funds-flow deficits of the early 1970s were checked, and improvements in RONA were sustained in every year but 1975, when the recession brought the company below its target. In addition, the corporate growth objective was held well below the rates actually achieved—perhaps to remind the managers that funds had to be generated to support the increased business.

The net effect of these changes was a sizable jump in the sustainable rate of growth, from 9 percent at the beginning of the period to 14 percent at the end. Within the constraints set by the discipline of the goals system, management's targets clearly migrated upward, as the company's performance confirmed its expectations. Moreover, this pattern of upward mobility was reinforced by the compensation incentives used in this and other companies. As we shall see, these plans replicate the goals system's emphasis on the maximization of corporate wealth. Thus their discipline over individual managers complements the discipline that the formal goals system exercises over the entire set of corporate financial goals.

Executive Compensation

Among the incentives that motivated senior management in these companies were status and position, power and influence, competitive success, and upward mobility. Financial rewards, which were an important but by no means dominant influence, mattered in their own right and as a proxy for other aspects of achievement. Thus they were apt to be seen as powerful signals of an individual manager's success or failure, particularly when they were directly related to areas over which the manager was believed to exercise control.

In most of the companies studied financial rewards had three components: a base salary, a bonus, and equity (in the form of stock options or a stock purchase plan). The first has few direct links to the financial goals system. Base salaries, in general, were loosely defined by the somewhat imperfect market for senior managers taken with factors such as industry norms, the size of the resource base to be managed, risk, the perceived uniqueness or scarcity of the managerial talents required, and the potential for influencing results. Similarly, the individual manager's salary was dominated by the established salary structure within the company and his or her ability to move up the corporate ladder.

In contrast, bonuses were calculated on the basis of performance criteria which were calibrated yearly. They were premised on the assumption that senior managers could materially influence results, in the short term as well as the long run, and their meaning went well beyond the immediate dollars involved (although these could be substantial, as bonuses typically ranged from 10 percent to 60 percent of base salary). Most important for our purposes, bonuses in these companies focus on criteria directly related to the maximization of corporate wealth.

Bonus plans typically referred to one dominant criterion, although they also incorporated a variety of refinements including level of responsibility, distinctions between corporate, divisional, and individual performance, multiple-year averaging, and other objective and subjective criteria. In seven of the twelve companies the dominant criterion for top-level bonus payments was growth in absolute earnings. An eighth company also focused on earnings, but its criterion was earnings per share, set at some specified target for the year (e.g., $3.00 to $4.00).

The four remaining companies used return on investment (corporate book value) as their dominant criterion; but only one, a conglomerate, applied it without qualification even at the divisional level. At the other companies more flexibility was apparent, and bonuses were influenced by management's desire to keep executive salaries significantly above the industry average or by specific strategic objectives. Under the latter plan, known as Management by Objectives and adhered to by two companies, divisional managers' bonuses were adjusted to reflect their success in penetrating specific product markets. Thus their compensation was closely linked to growth and the product-market constituency as well as to ROI.

Before turning to the third component of the compensation package, it is important to point out that in practical terms it made little difference whether ROI or growth in absolute earnings was used as the bonus criterion. In the abstract, of course, a distinction exists, because the for-mer refers to the quality of earnings while the latter refers to quantity. Further, there is a real danger in focusing on ROI too strongly at the divisional level, where it can restrict investment options in established product markets and damage future returns. But in most of these com-panies strategic planning was undertaken with the clear understanding that the investment base would continue to grow. Thus it was assumed that growth in absolute earnings would be enhanced, if ROI improved. The two criteria were complementary, when applied with common sense.

Interestingly, at the time of this study, even the conglomerate's man-agement had begun to rethink its reliance on a pure ROI criterion. Charging that the standard had led to creative accounting and a preoccu-pation with short-term results, several top managers were pressing for a new formula that would emphasize long-term performance as well as re-turns. Their experience reminds us that executive compensation systems, like financial goals, undergo periodic review, as managements change di-rection or seek fresh stimuli for corporate performance.

Executive stock options and purchase plans, the remaining compo-nent of the compensation package, also reinforced management's dual concern for earnings and growth. This was so, even though it is widely assumed that the managers' ownership stake gives them a close sense of identity with the shareholders and therefore a paramount interest in the company's earnings. However, as has been noted, the particular category of shareholders with whom this identity is formed is a special one: the long-term, undiversified, loyal shareholders whose personal wealth is in-timately bound up with the growth of *this* corporation's wealth and who share management's faith in its future. Consequently, management tends to credit the stockholders with its own interest in corporate wealth as measured by growth in earnings. As one chief executive observed:

> We have not emphasized in this company market value of the stock as
> much as some companies have. . . . If over the long run we do a good
> job, it will be reflected in the market value of the stock. . . . We look
> long term. . . . [Analysts] can't understand cycles or technology so we
> have to run the company our way to provide excitement, growth, and
> richness. . . . There should be ways to *attract stockholders who have the*
> *long-term on their mind and who think like management.* The same way
> you have to get around the union to talk to the workers, so you have
> to get around the analyst to talk to the investors. (Emphasis added.)

Of course, some managers do pay serious attention to equity market values, price-earnings ratios, and other capital-market signals. A few may even believe that smaller can be better. But the overwhelming evidence of this study indicates that most do not. On the contrary, the sign of corporate success—and the pathway to it—is growth in earnings and in *reinvested* earnings.

Although the relation between financial rewards and motivation is beyond the scope of this study, the relation between particular compensation schemes and specific goals deserves consideration. On funding issues the links between compensation schemes and particular choices are indirect at best, in part because these schemes are primarily designed for operating managers who have little involvement in these matters. The incentives commonly used do lend implicit support to the principle of financial self-sufficiency, because they emphasize growth in absolute earnings, including internally generated funds which are the major source of continuous funding. But they do not address the source of funds directly, nor are they relevant to capital-structure issues such as the tradeoff between debt leverage and dividend payout or the desirable amount of each.

Links between compensation and specific choices are more evident when the goals involved relate to aspects of the system over which operating managers exercise some control such as volume, price, cost, and investment. Indeed, corporate records indicate that a strong and persistent emphasis on growth in absolute earnings tends to influence managers' choices and performance in two ways. On one hand, they tilt the diagonal line of self-sufficiency as far upward as possible, to gain the maximum growth for any given RONA. On the other, they move the target goals out along the line as far as it is realistically possible to go. They do so because they believe that the company's absolute earnings will be enhanced by both the growth in the volume of business transacted and by management's increased effectiveness in translating profit on sales into RONA (through higher profits on sales, a higher sales-to-assets ratio, or a higher assets-to-net assets ratio).

On the basis of this evidence we can reasonably conclude that the executive incentive systems in these companies were fundamentally consistent with the financial goals system.[3] However, neither compensation systems nor financial goals alone can illuminate such critical issues as the adequacy and riskiness of the total funding strategy or the stability and sustainability of corporate earnings. To explore these questions management must be able to assess corporate performance in the light of its long-term objectives. Tracking provides one useful tool for this assessment process.

Monitoring Performance Against Financial Goals

Figure 7-2 presents a model for tracking and interpreting corporate performance against goals. The model is based on the familiar graph of the self-sustaining growth equation together with the point which repre-

Figure 7:2   A Model For Monitoring Performance Against Goals

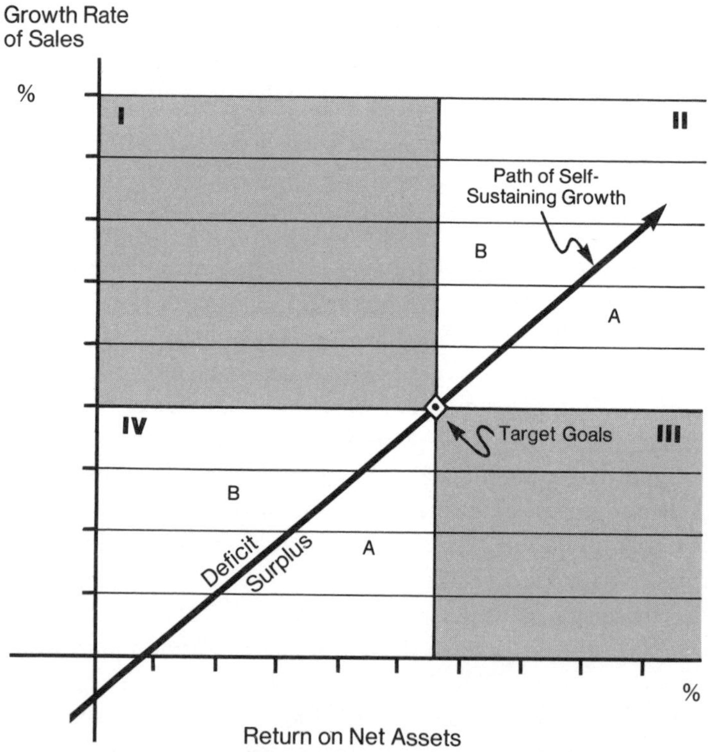

Quadrant I: Superior Growth, Inferior RONA
Quadrant II: Absolutely Superior Performance
Quadrant III: Inferior Growth, Superior RONA
Quadrant IV: Absolutely Inferior Performance
Note: A = Sustainable Performance
        B = Unsustainable Performance

sents an ideal financial goals system for the company in question. As the reader will remember, this point defines a target growth rate, a rate of return on net assets, an earnings-retention ratio, and a debt-equity ratio. The space of the graph is then further divided into four quadrants centered on that point or composite financial target. As can be seen, Quadrants II and IV are bisected by the self-sustaining growth line, so that performance in these quadrants may produce a deficit or surplus of funds depending on the side of the line on which it falls.

Actual performance represented by a point falling in Quadrant II is absolutely superior in terms of both the rate of growth and the rate of return. If the point lies in Sector IIA, this superior performance can be sustained; if it lies in Sector IIB, it is inherently unsustainable. In contrast, Quadrant IV performance is absolutely inferior on both counts, although it, too, can be assessed for sustainability. In the remaining quadrants deliberate or inadvertent tradeoffs exist between the goals for growth and for return on investment. Quadrant I performance reflects superior growth coupled with an inferior return on net assets. It is unsustainable in the long run. Conversely, Quadrant III performance reflects inferior growth and a superior return on net assets. In the long run this performance is financially sustainable because it tends to produce a surplus of funds flows.

Using this tracking model, Figure 7-3 plots Company B's performance against its goals for the nine-year period from 1970–78. During these years the company was engaged in continuing efforts to develop new product markets to replace its maturing income streams. Because these efforts were undertaken well before the traditional markets had aged severely, the company did not have to cycle through Quadrants IV and I before achieving absolutely superior performance. Instead superior RONA and growth performance anchored it securely in Quadrants II and III. The company surpassed the RONA target every year but one, and it exceeded the target for growth in five years out of the nine. (Two of the years showing inferior growth occurred during general business recessions.)

However, the trend toward higher rates of growth and somewhat lower rates of return, evident in the company's performance track record, tended to place it in an unsustainable cash-flow position. This trend was understandable, given the internal product-development program. Still, the funds-flow implications had to be addressed. As we see, management acknowledged funds-flow realities in its goals, which targeted deficits throughout the period. The targeted growth rate increased considerably, presumably in response to performance. But the RONA target remained constant, influenced, perhaps, by the impact of experience, which sug-

Figure 7:3 Company B: Record of Performance, 1970-78

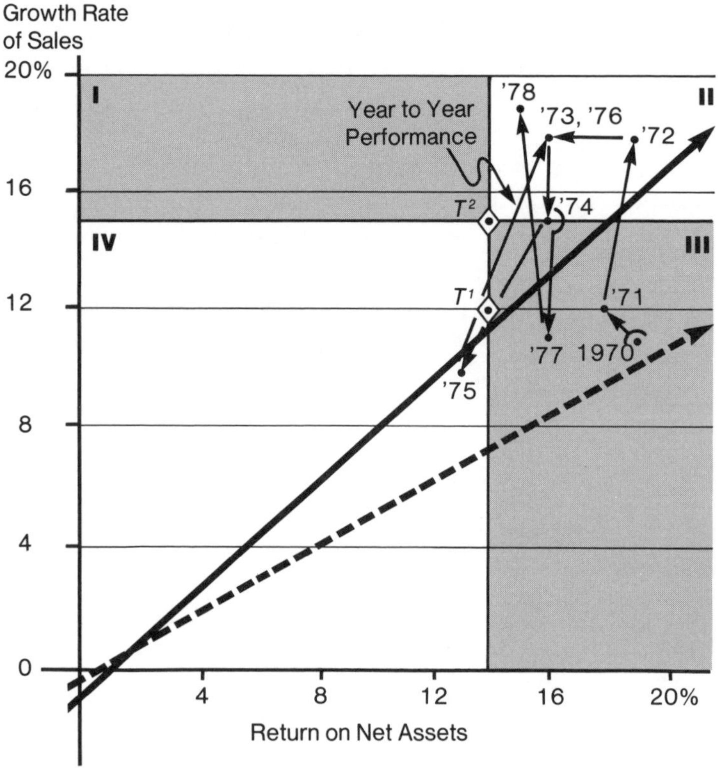

T¹ = Original Targets for Growth and RONA
T² = Current Targets for Growth and RONA
Broken Line = Path of Self-Sustaining Growth with Original Goals (T¹)
Solid Line = Path of Self-Sustaining Growth with Current Goals (T²)

gested that returns were declining, at least in the near term, and by management's reluctance to foster undue optimism about the new product
markets' prospects.

Management turned to several sources to fund these deficits, including an improved sales-to-assets ratio and an increased earnings-retention
ratio. Because the company is privately held, equity offerings were not an
available option here, as they were at Company A. However, the debt-
equity ratio represented a major funds-flow asset. By shifting the com-

pany's use of debt from zero to more than 25 percent of equity, management gained a substantial one-time increase in corporate funds and the leverage to sustain a higher rate of growth. The effects of this policy change, together with the higher earnings-retention ratio, are evident in the exhibit. The slope of the self-sustaining growth line was raised to such an extent that the company's actual performance was consistent with a funds-flow surplus in four of the nine years, and the sustainable growth rate increased from approximately 6 percent to 11 percent.

Company B's strong record stands in striking contrast to Company C's performance during the same period (Figure 7-4). This management was also trying to diversify out of a mature product market. But its acquisition choices only intensified the cyclicality of the historic industry base. Volume contracted sharply during the recessions with results that are apparent in the company's track record: valleys and peaks replace the clockwise rotation toward superior performance evident in Company A's results (see Figure 7-1).

As Figure 7-4 indicates, the company struggled throughout the decade to escape from the gloom of Quadrant IV's absolutely inferior performance relative to goals to Quadrant I, where growth was superior though unsustainable, because of insufficient returns. The modest trend toward a higher return on investment gave management some grounds to hope that the company's performance would eventually reach Quadrant II. But thus far, success had eluded its grasp.

The movement in the corporate goals system evident in the other exhibits cannot be documented in this case, because the company's goals at the beginning of the period were largely qualitative. Current targets would generate a modest surplus of funds, but the company's experience was far from fulfilling these expectations. Instead, for most of the decade there was a funds-flow deficit, which the company survived through various means. Debt leverage remained constant and relatively high throughout the period. A moderate amount of equity was used for acquisitions. Modest improvements were achieved in the sales-to-assets ratio. And—most significantly—the dividend payout declined substantially. Ignoring bulges created by the recession, when earnings dropped dramatically, the payout fell from 54 percent in 1969 to 24 percent in 1978.

Before leaving this presentation of corporate goals, a word of caution about corporate management's apparent single-mindedness and clear vision is in order. On the one hand, goals must be boldly stated and clearly defined to influence organizational behavior. On the other hand, top management possesses neither second sight nor such finely tuned corporate controls that it can alter course quickly and accurately. Conse-

Figure 7:4 Company C: Record of Performance, 1969-78

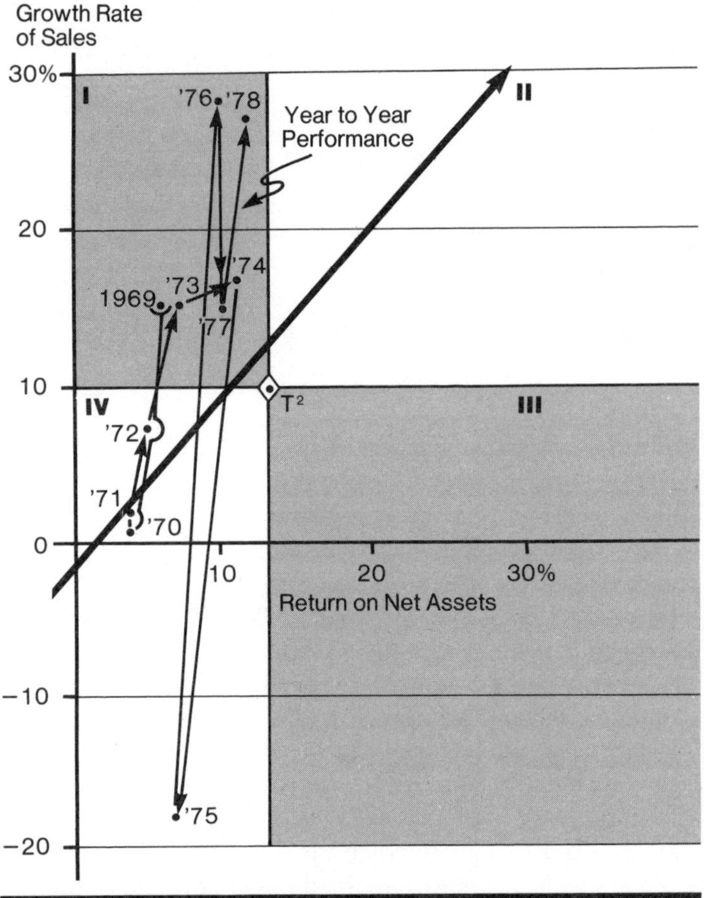

Growth Rate
of Sales

T^2 = Current Targets for Growth and RONA
Solid Line = Path of Self-Sustaining Growth with Current Goals

quently, there are bound to be differences of opinion within management about which goals ought to dominate, particularly when they concern the short-term conflict between growth and return on investment.

The dimensions of this real world dilemma were sketched out by one executive as he reflected on his company's recent history:

In the early seventies there were a lot of issues that were not resolved. The basic conflict was between financial strength and performance on the one hand and growth on the other. [Mr. X], chairman of our Finance Committee, was very strong on financial performance. [Mr. Y] thought that the company had to emphasize growth. The management didn't even agree on individual goals.

Growth to [Mr. X] represented a commodity business. He argued for technological leadership and growth would take care of itself. But the ballgame changed and our competition changed. Business became more competitive. We became conscious of product life cycles and the need to sustain a strong market position. We had to finance growth in order to stay in the competitive race. At one time the company had an ROI hurdle rate of 20% after taxes, a standard developed and enforced by [Mr. X]. The net result was that we reduced debt substantially and accumulated cash. The company was profitable and financially strong and that was a form of success that was hard to argue with. However, things began to go downhill—we began losing ground to competitors. . . . Now we have a target growth rate and a different ROI target which is a function of that growth—a credible target to shoot at.

In this instance Mr. X's target was both hard to argue with and wrong in terms of the company's future health and vitality. By using a model such as the one presented here, management might have been able to anticipate the lessons experience was about to teach. Yet, even so, its judgments would have been relative to the specific set of goals already in place. Consequently, it is particularly important to explore the forces that influence those choices in the short run.

Locating the Target: The Immediate Future

Year-to-year records of corporate performance against goals indicate that a company rarely—if ever—hits its target bull's eye. Nevertheless, this point, collectively defined by the key financial goals, is critical to corporate strategy because it identifies the area in which management will concentrate its firepower. In the long run, as we have discovered, management should set its sights on a point which falls along the line that defines a balanced funds-flow and financial self-sufficiency. But as we have also seen, managements often deliberately vary from this mark because they plan to consume, or generate, financial reserves for a time. Consequently, their corporate goals shift over time, moving up or down, above or below the line.

What governs this movement? Is the target's location determined by consensus? By the CEO? By forces beyond management's control? Our evidence points to the last: *In the short run, at least, forces beyond management's immediate control determine the target's location.* Constituents' demands, the business environment, the company's actual performance record, the availability of funds: these are the factors that constrain management as it chooses its key financial goals.

Figure 7-5 presents management's discretionary zone in the form of a rectangle that boxes off a portion of the now-familiar line defining growth

Figure 7:5   Locating the Target Goals: Short Run
Boundaries on Choice

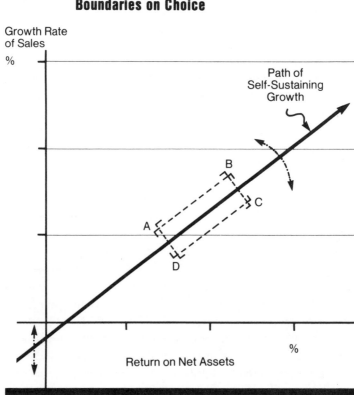

rate and RONA combinations that produce a relative balance in funds flows (that is, the line of self-sufficiency). Arrows indicate the boundaries to remind us that they are not hard and fast. Rather, they represent outer limits set by the forces beyond management's immediate control which bound both the location and slope of the line and the position on or near it of the corporation's financial goals system.

As previously noted, the earnings-retention ratio and the debt-equity ratio determine the slope and position of the self-sufficient growth line. In a company with neither debt nor dividends this line passes through the origin at a 45° angle, so that every value of RONA will continuously fund an equivalent rate of growth. The slope declines and the potential for sustained growth is diminished to the extent that shareholders extract some portion of earnings for consumption or alternative investment. Conversely, the slope and the potential for sustained growth increase to the extent that lenders are willing to fund some fraction of the firm's long-term capital base. Aggressive management will therefore tend to push both earnings retention and debt leverage as far as the capital market's tolerance allows. At that point the position of the line stabilizes by reason of the shareholders' preference for payouts and the lenders' preference for prudent debt-equity limits.

The target's lower bound (A ↔ D) is set by the organizational demand for growth and/or the present and projected rates of growth for the industry or industries in which the firm operates. Of these, the latter is the more inexorable. To set a growth objective below the industry's minimum rate is to concede territory deliberately to competitors. No management will make this choice unless it is consciously engaged in harvesting, and even then it will apply only to selected segments of the corporate product-market portfolio. For the company as a whole the overriding importance of maintaining or improving market share establishes an industry-defined floor for growth.

The upper bound for corporate growth (B ↔ C) is set by management's analysis of the opportunities for increasing market share and improving return on investment and by its perception of what is realistically attainable within the planning horizon. Hence it is less precisely defined and depends significantly on how aggressive management is in seeking to gain market share from its competitors. Nevertheless, factors beyond management's control constrain its corporate ambitions. These include the industry environment and economic climate as well as the company's past and current performance and that of its primary competitors. A mature company with a large share of market may find further expansion difficult for economic, competitive, or political reasons. Business cycles and secular trends may also limit opportunities, and they will surely condition management's expectations. Similarly, management must reckon with its own company's performance—and the industry's—if its growth and RONA goals are to maintain credibility and discipline subordinate managers.

The final element in management's choice of a target is its position relative to the line: Can management safely target a deficit or a surplus of funds for the planning period? In this context constraints are set by the level at which corporate resources are currently being utilized. Excess capacity will support an above-the-line target for a time, whereas overcommitted resources require a below-the-line target to build up flexibility in the resource base. Further, it bears repeating that these resources include the relative efficiency of the human and financial working assets in place as well as redundant liquid assets or unused debt capacity. In other words, these issues are both financial and, importantly, managerial or organizational. Thus management's freedom to set goals will be significantly affected by the commitment of those within and without the firm to its operation.

Managing Goals at the Strategic Business Unit Level

Companies succeed or fail in their economic functions at the divisional level. Specific competitors are confronted by the individual divisions or strategic business units (SBUs), and their managers generate many, if not most, of the company's established product-market investment options. Consequently, divisional performance is vitally important to the overall record of corporate performance against goals. In addition, divisional goals and guidelines provide a primary test of the corporate goals system's disciplinary power. Have corporate management's goals been effectively translated at the divisional level—or does the goals system lose its coherence among the company's individual parts?

The most significant difference between corporate plans and goals and those found at the divisional level lies in their constituency focus. SBU managers are closest to the product market. Preoccupied with the competitive dynamics of individual product markets, they are highly sensitive to the priorities of customers, suppliers, competitors, and the work force. Moreover, this sensitivity is clearly reflected in the form and substance of their goals, which tend to stress growth and competitive presence in preference to capital-market concerns.

A study commissioned in 1976 by one of the companies in preparation for an upcoming management conference illustrates operating managers' concerns. Seventy executives were polled anonymously by a nationally renowned opinion-survey company. Eighty-five percent responded by submitting lists of the matters most on their minds. Over half cited the same ten topics as their highest priority. The top four were: ways to future growth; the ability of the company to withstand technological challenge from competitors; criteria for allocating resources; and the need for major diversification. The next four dealt with organizational issues, such as the adequacy of the organizational structure; the last two reflected product-market concerns as well: the competitive and economic environment five to ten years hence, and the need to analyze unique corporate strength.

All these topics relate to survival and success in the product-market arena and to competitive and organizational prerequisites. However, financial or funding issues surface only in the third item: how each SBU would be assured its fair share of capital resources. Moreover, this inattention to capital-market issues characterizes the list as a whole. Of fifty-two topics only three dealt with financial matters: the rationale for corporate financial policies (number 16); headquarter requirements for financial data (number 45); and relationships with the financial community (number 51). And as is obvious, even these had strong organizational overtones as well.

In contrast, external funding issues and the external capital market are continuing concerns among top managements in well-established corporations. Consequently, there can be a latent (or explicit) tension between top management's capital-market emphasis and the divisional managers' emphasis on growth. Just such a tension resonates in the following statement, made by a division head as he outlined a new set of divisional goals. (To give the complete context the statement is reported in full.)

> Outlined in the box below are recently-stated goals for the Unit. They are perhaps not so simple as some would like or as specific as others would prefer. They do, however, reflect the environment in which we operate today and expect for the future. These are intended as "umbrella" goals for the Unit, and it is expected supporting Functional, Product, and Organization goals will be developed as appropriate.

You will note that *profit has clearly replaced volume as our primary concern*. This reflects the tie between profitability, capital availability, growth, and job security.

While it is perhaps not necessary to be a volume leader in every product category, we do believe that a major market-share position is necessary to achieve the efficiencies and low-cost position which, in turn, provide profit opportunity. Thus, while our primary goal is profitability, volume in selected major products is expected to be a major tool in reaching that goal.

Because reaching these goals is essential to the health and success of the Unit, and each of us as individuals, measurement of results and reports of progress will be made on a continuous basis.

Your support of this profitability leadership goal is sincerely requested, and your personal opportunities and benefits clearly tied to its attainment.

SBU PERFORMANCE GOALS

[This SBU's] primary goal is to produce a level of profitability which preserves the owners' [shareholders'] assets, provides long-term job security for employees, attracts sufficient capital to grow in sales and earnings, and meets corporate goals and objectives. Success will be measured by comparing unit performance with the top three industry competitors and with that of the Corporation. The key areas of comparison will be Return on Assets and sustained sales and profit growth.

It is also our goal to concentrate Research, Capital Expenditures, and Market Development programs in areas that build on our strengths or provide balance to our base products and industries served.

While pursuing these goals, we will fulfill our legal and moral responsibilities in all dealings with employees, customers, suppliers, and the communities where we operate—and go the extra steps required to insure a tie-breaking edge in elective decisions made by people evaluating us.

Even though this statement declares that profits are the division's "primary concern," volume and growth are clearly its dominant themes. Moreover, the product-market perspective they reflect appears elsewhere in the statement as well. For example, in listing the uses of profitability, preservation of the shareholders' assets comes first; but, just as important, if not more so, are the jobs and growth profits assure. Similarly, when the corporation's legal and moral duties to its constituents are assessed, shareholders are not even mentioned. Last, but not least, it is top industry competitors who define successful operations and establish relevant performance criteria. Other divisions within the corporate entity take a backseat to traditional product-market rivals.

Given the strength of this product-market perspective at the divisional or SBU level, it is not surprising that the corporate self-sustaining growth line tends to be taken as a given, if only because it relates to debt and dividend policies which these managers cannot control. They concentrate, instead, on getting and sustaining growth and profitability, both of which are seen to flow, in the short run at least, from control of a defined, established product-market position. Nevertheless, in the scramble among competing SBUs for limited financial and human resources, performance above or below the self-sustaining growth line strongly influences an individual unit's chances for success.

Financial self-sufficiency is not always an appropriate criterion, however. To assume that all new product-market initiatives will be transformed into full competitive vigor and financial independence within a year or two flies in the face of common sense. It is much more likely that new SBUs will pass through a life cycle comparable to that of the corporation as a whole. As Figure 7-6 illustrates, this cycle can be broken down into five separate stages. During the first or entry phase the SBU's rate of growth and return are typically lower than desired, and the latter may even be negative for a time. As momentum builds and sales improve, the SBU moves upward and to the right into the first quadrant, where growth is superior although returns are still under target. If the product is successfully established, the SBU continues its cycle into Quadrant II, where all corporate goals are more than satisfied (Stage 3). Thereafter, although growth declines as the product-market matures (Stage 4), superior returns are realized from its substantial market share until the SBU enters its last, or harvest, stage. At this point, which may be decades after the product's introduction, inferior growth and RONA lead to the SBU's termination and its replacement in the corporate portfolio by new initiatives.[4]

The point, of course, is that it is unrealistic to expect that all SBUs will be in a self-sustaining mode at any given time. Some new entry positions will require a substantial financial subsidy for extended periods. Other product markets will generate more funds than they can sensibly reinvest. What is essential to corporate strategy is that *the corporate portfo-*

Figure 7:6   Generalized Individual Product Market Life Cycle

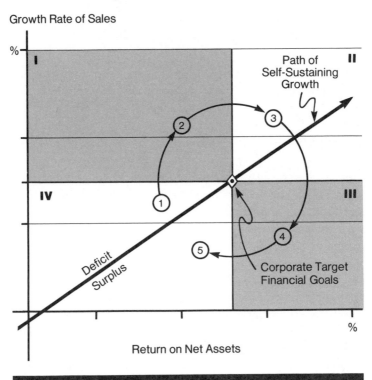

Growth Rate of Sales

lio be balanced, so that the corporation as a whole is a self-sufficient product and capital market. A first or second stage SBU must have access to
the excess funds provided by an SBU that has matured or begun to be
harvested. Mix and timing are therefore critical to corporate strategic
success.

Many managements already recognize their SBUs' financial interdependence and the need for balance in the corporate portfolio. The following statement of SBU-level objectives is taken from one company's planning documents for the three-year period from 1978 to 1981. As the
reader will see, its product-market development phases correspond to the
SBU life cycle stages marked off in Figure 7-6.

- For a New Entity
  - (a) Successfully launch [brand name] to achieve 6% market share
  - (b) Develop new products

- For a Newly Established Product
  - (a) Produce increased operating profit in each plan year
  - (b) Hold [brand name] at 20% market share

- For an Established Product Market
  - (a) Improve operating profit
  - (b) Hold Number Two market position

- For a Mature Product: (Declining Growth)
  - (a) Maximize profitability
  - (b) Increase consumption
  - (c) Hold market position

- For a Harvest Mode
  - (a) Harvest [brand name] for profit
  - (b) Explore new products

These objectives follow a logical progression in terms of management's expectations for profitability and product-market growth. On the one hand, management's profit objectives are clearly keyed to the relative maturity of the company's branded products. Profits receive no emphasis at the point of entry, but they are a dominant concern in an SBU's later days, when expenditures related to future demand are cut off completely. (During the stages in between entry and harvest, profitability is expected to rise along a qualitative ladder which moves from increase to improvement to maximization.) On the other hand, market share is also a major objective in every phase but the harvest mode. Depending on the maturity of their respective SBUs, managers are urged to establish, increase, or hold their market position, with obvious implications for their target rates of growth.

Not all managements shared this balanced view of product-market life cycles, however. At some companies, SBUs were expected to achieve financial self-sufficiency almost immediately or face the consequences. Executives from two different companies put the matter bluntly, saying:

> A common thread is that each business unit, with few exceptions, is expected to operate at a level which will produce enough cash to finance its own needs. These self-sustaining performance goals are a necessity.

The chief financial officer has presented the concept of self-sustaining goals to the division managers. He has provided the data to show whether the various divisions are supporting their own sales growth objectives. Not being self-sufficient has been characterized as a sign of second-class citizenship.

In weighing the merits of these statements, which seem to leave no room for financially disadvantaged SBUs, we need to distinguish between the disciplinary and predictive functions of goals. In the former context they are meant to elicit superior performance by motivating the organization. In the latter goals are meant to provide realistic measures of management's expectations. Financial self-sufficiency for every SBU all of the time is an unrealistic expectation in most companies. But it presents a very different prospect when seen as a long-term goal well worth striving for.

Short Run, Long Run

This chapter has been devoted to the management of a financial goals system in the short run, that is, the normal three- to five-year planning horizon over which its underlying assumptions are assumed to hold. During this period the established firm confronts a set of external and internal constraints that must be taken as given: a defined capital-market constituency, a specific set of products, known product markets and competitors, an established organization and set of human resources, and a level of financial resources and resource utilization produced by management's past decisions and corporate experience. Consequently, *the relevant financial goals system for any given company is in large measure set for management—not by it.* In the near term management's options are boxed within what may be very narrow limits not of its own current choosing.

In the long run this need not be the case. Some or all of these constraints may be relaxed to provide an opportunity for greater freedom of choice. Over a longer time line, such as that typified by a successful chief executive's normal tenure in office, management can aspire to set a course more nearly its own. How this happens is the subject of the last chapter, which examines a range of strategies whereby management can gain greater control over its internal and external environment.

Notes

1. The reader is reminded that the self-sustaining growth equation can be graphed as a line, which defines the return on investment necessary for any given target growth rate to be consistent with the principle of self-sustaining growth (i.e., growth funded through retained earnings and their increment of new debt). A target represented by a point anywhere above the line (e.g., T_1) implies a planned deficit in funds flows, while a target represented by a point anywhere below the line (e.g., T_2) implies a planned surplus in funds flows. The slope of the line representing self-sustaining growth is defined by the company's funding strategy: its target rate of earnings retention coupled with the related debt-equity ratio. For a fuller explanation see Chapter 4.

2. Diversification by acquisition and its relation to the funding of established product markets will be discussed in Chapter 8.

3. For an example of a compensation system explicitly linked to the self-sufficient goals system, see Ray Stata and Modesto A. Madique, "Bonus System for Balanced Strategy." *Harvard Business Review* 58 (November–December 1980): 156–63.

4. Obvious similarities exist between the Boston Consulting Group's two-by-two grid, which defines the corporate life cycle in terms of industry growth rate and share of market, and which classifies SBUs on a learning curve of growth and profitability as "stars," "cows," or "dogs," and this model—the more so because most of the companies studied were dedicated to a share-of-market philosophy. However, the financial goals-system model is purely financial and says nothing about the origins of superior returns. It provides a device for plotting individual SBU performance against the corporate goals system, and it highlights the SBU's financial interdependence and the need for balance in the portfolio.

8

Strategies for Managerial Independence

The Roots of Constituency Power

Even the most talented leader of a large corporation faces certain givens. National and international economies, social and political environments, the course of the business cycle, the underlying economic forces of the industries in which the company operates: none of these can be changed single-handedly. Corporate history and performance records cannot be rewritten; nor can people's perceptions of that history be easily changed. Nevertheless, important dimensions of the corporate environment can be altered, given enough time, talent, and commitment. In particular, top management can develop strategies that affect the composition and power of the capital market, product market, and organizational constituencies on which the company's survival depends. Thus it can hope to redraw the boundaries set by these constituencies which collectively define the near-term choice of corporate goals.

For the most part each constituency's power derives from the fact that it supplies vital resources and opportunities which it can limit or withhold if an individual corporation fails to satisfy its self-interest. For example, managers ordinarily have a degree of freedom in choosing the operative debt-equity ratio which influences the slope of the company's self-sustaining growth line. But that freedom can be reduced or eliminated if the lenders are troubled by corporate performance. By reducing the flow of debt capital through debt limits or restrictive covenants, the lenders lower the line's slope and thereby lower the company's rate of growth for any given rate of return on net assets. (Alternatively, the lenders' actions can be seen in terms of raising the required return on net assets for any given rate of growth.)

Shareholders restrict the flow of resources to the corporation in a similar manner when they require a larger fraction of current earnings for consumption or alternative investment. Thus increased dividend payouts have similar consequences for corporate growth potential as reductions in debt leverage. But because shareholders are typically a dispersed and diverse group, their power is less focused and direct than that of key lenders and their collective preferences are less apparent. Customarily rather passive, they tend to express their disapproval by selling their stock without sending management a clear message about what has displeased them. Consequently, the managers have considerable latitude in the timing and extent of their response, even when, for example, they are convinced (as many were in the late 1970s) that the stock market is placing increased emphasis on dividend income.

Of course the shareholders' primary power lies in their ability to become activists by exercising their franchise and participating in efforts to depose the existing management. Management is certainly aware of this potential, and it is always on the alert for evidence of moves by or on behalf of dissident shareholders. However, it is almost impossible to define the link between management's perception of the shareholders' expectations for dividends and market value on the one hand, and the shareholders' perception of management's ability to fulfill their expectations on the other. In the aftermath of a battle for control the links may become more evident, because the issues that arise in such battles often cover the entire spectrum of management's performance, including the central dimensions of the financial goals system. But which particular funding strategies or tradeoffs between growth and rate of return would make for a passive (or supportive) shareholder population cannot be predicted in advance. Under normal circumstances, therefore, the shareholders appear to allow a relatively broad range of managerial discretion.

In the product-market constituency power is exercised primarily through competitive interaction, as we have seen. The existence of strong rivals disciplines individual managements to promote essential growth and investment and to constrain profit or returns on investment. In addition, corporate funding options are likely to be strongly influenced by key competitors' strategies, even though the product-market constituency is traditionally silent on funding questions and a range of acceptable choices exists. This is so because management often looks to its competitors to measure the extent to which they can (or cannot) leverage equity with debt or retain earnings for reinvestment. To the extent that a company achieves industry dominance and leadership, it may acquire greater control over the pace of industry investment and the rate of return. And yet, ironically, in the long run a leadership position may also strengthen the company's dependency on its industry performance and make it more, rather than less, sensitive to product-market priorities.

When management refers to its organization, it tends to exclude that segment of the corporate work force, best illustrated by but not limited to unionized labor, which delivers a standardized unit or service at a market rate. Instead the term is applied to the supervisory personnel, technical staff, and line management whose individual and collective ability, experience, and initiative can make the difference between corporate failure and success. Top management identifies with these key employees. It relies on them for the follow-through to implement its decisions. It believes that their continuing loyalty is vital to the accomplishment of the company's business mission. In addition, top management's concern for its organization is accentuated by the trend toward a managerial profession and by the perception that the most talented personnel are highly mobile.

To attract and hold a talented organization, therefore, management works hard to create the best possible working environment. In practice this means that it seeks to provide the right mix of stimulating work, upward mobility, job security, financial rewards, and recognition. Because experience confirms the widespread belief that these needs are most readily met when the company is growing, they have a considerable impact on corporate goals and strategy. In fact, in the companies studied organizational priorities ultimately dominated corporate strategy and provided the impetus for the drive to diversify out of mature product markets into new and more rapidly growing ones. Through such moves managements sought to ensure that their companies would grow steadily at a rate equal to or better than their competitors and that they would generate sufficient earnings to support that growth and provide adequate rewards.

The fact that conflicts can arise among the needs and interests of the several constituencies has already been discussed. Thus, even in the short term, management must work to assure tradeoffs in the company's goals and performance which will retain all the constituencies' cooperation—if not their spontaneous loyalty. Nevertheless, even as these tradeoffs are made, management is watchful of constituency attempts to limit its prerogatives. Academics may label managers as agents and explain their behavior in terms of agency theory; but most top managers regard themselves as leaders, not followers, and their constituencies figure prominently among those they mean to lead. As leaders they have their own view of the corporation's mission, goals, and strategies, independent of those held by existing constituencies and possibly at variance with them. And as leaders, they seek to assume an independent role in setting corporate goals and resolving conflicts, by developing strategies that expand their range of effective choices.

Before considering these strategies and their impact on the financial goals system, it is important to emphasize the purpose of this discussion. The sections that follow are meant to describe the strategies in question and show their potential for giving management a greater degree of control over financial goals systems. They do not take a position on the social or economic merits of the strategies, which propose to circumvent the disciplines imposed on individual managements by the various public markets for corporate resources. Whether society as a whole benefits or suffers when managers expand their range of choice relative to shareholders, customers, or employees can be debated. But an accurate description of the modern corporate business entity must precede that debate.

Strategies for Expanding Managerial Choice: The Capital Markets

Financial self-sufficiency is management's primary strategy for relaxing the capital market's discipline over its organization. As we have seen, this strategy seeks to forestall conditions under which the capital markets can exercise maximum leverage over the company's goals. By relying on internal equity funding and a conservative, arm's length debt policy, it is designed to ensure that the corporation will never have to come to the market to fund a vital strategic need that cannot be deferred. When the strategy is successful, management controls the use of these resources totally and avoids all negotiations with external parties.

If a company frequently pushes against the limits of its borrowing capacity or its earning retention for relief from undercapitalization, as is the case in some regulated industries, its management will have to be more sensitive to investors' current preferences, particularly those of the professionals whose horizons are often much shorter than career managers think appropriate. Therefore, given a choice, the typical nonregulated industry manager is likely to opt for a smaller amount of capital, which he can control completely and on which he or she can plan with confidence, rather than a larger amount subject to more negotiation with external parties and less certain in magnitude and timing.

As a group the research sample was highly successful in implementing a strategy of financial self-sufficiency from the late 1960s through the 1970s. During this period these companies achieved substantial and sustained growth through such funding. In addition, the strategy gave the companies' managements considerable leeway in their investment decisions. Two of the three basic elements of these decisions—the choice of product markets and the investment mix—were entirely within management's prerogatives, while the third, the amount to be invested, was primarily a function of earnings performance, although it was loosely constrained by the prevailing dividend policy norms and more directly affected by the lenders' perceptions of safe debt limits.

Generalizing these companies' experiences with financial self-sufficiency is problematic. Some observers may conclude that it represents a unique historical event: the result of a sustained period of general economic buoyancy which gave the managers a once-in-a-lifetime freedom from capital-market forces. Therefore, they would argue that industrial managements should not hope to escape the discipline of capital-market preferences under ordinary economic conditions (i.e., a world of capital scarcity in which public and private institutions compete for corporate and individual savings).

If this analysis is correct, the 1980s will be particularly challenging because American industrial managements will also be faced with the problem of replacing their established asset bases at greatly inflated prices. Indeed, as they look forward to a strong and sustained recovery period, many managements have already begun to recognize that this attrition, coupled with the drain of inflated interest costs, has left their companies undercapitalized. Evidence of this thinking has already appeared in the flurry of new equity issues that accompanied the stock market's rebound in 1983. But it remains to be seen whether American industry can finance the next decade with as little dependence on the capital market as in the 1970s—and what difference, if any, this will make in management's financial priorities.

A second strategy for achieving independence from the capital markets focuses on the use of slack within the corporate system. As we have seen, this slack takes many forms, including the purely financial ones of liquid reserves and unused debt capacity. In addition, excess capacity in the corporation's economic and human resources provides the potential for substantial improvements in sales-to-assets ratios. Past investment patterns may place the firm at the leading edge of industry technology and state-of-the-art production. Market share and competitive dominance affect its ability to lay back for a time, without losing market presence. Key employees' commitment and goodwill can lead to superior performance and a sharper competitive edge. Thus individually and in combination, these factors help companies achieve higher rates of growth than those their current rates of return would seem to allow.

However, neither financial reserves nor organizational slack lasts forever. The growth they support cannot be sustained indefinitely, and management must recognize this fact when it commits these resources to productive use. Moreover, the gains expected from consuming reserves in pursuit of a known opportunity must be weighed against the risk of leaving the company inadequately defended against unexpected adversities.[1] For example, in many of the companies studied, slack was used to assist in funding product-market diversification without relying on the external capital market. However, the risk in this strategy lay in the possibility that the diversification would not be completed and consolidated before a serious economic recession tested the strength of the new earnings base. Thus the use—and restoration—of financial slack was a key managerial issue in these companies.

The issue of control over the decision-making process lies at the heart of management's capital-market strategies. As has been noted, the threat posed by lenders' restrictive debt-contract covenants was relatively easily contained by the adoption of conservative debt policies which kept the companies' lenders at arm's length. However, actual or potential challenges from enfranchised shareholders presented corporate managers with a more complex problem.

Ironically, the managers of totally private companies were the most free to downplay shareholders' priorities in their financial goals. For example, the decision to sacrifice short-term shareholder benefits (by cutting the dividend payout or accepting depressed earnings for an extended period) could be made instantaneously by one or two persons, providing flexibility that was the envy of their peers in publicly held companies. Similarly, these private companies provided the clearest examples of managements committed to preserving corporate wealth through long-term product-market transformations which would assure the organization's survival and thereby perpetuate family control.

Neither of these findings was anticipated when the study was first conceived. On the contrary, it was assumed that concentrated ownership would produce the clearest, most unequivocal expression of stockholder interest and that this interest would tend to dominate the company's financial goals system because the owners were the ultimate authority. Both assumptions proved to have limited explanatory value, however, even though the private companies (and the public companies in which members of the management team held unusual concentrations of voting stock) included individuals whose authority was consolidated through ownership and whose opinions on the stockholders' interests represented the last word. For one thing, it was by no means clear that the owner-managers exercised their power on behalf of the investors. Further, the need to accommodate investors' goals to those of the product-market and organizational constituencies was most apparent in the totally private companies because they lacked the option of turning to the public equity market when internal funds ran out.

In the publicly held companies most managements have very imperfect information about their shareholders' preferences. Individual owners are difficult, it not impossible, to identify and classify; for the most part they are silent on issues such as mission and strategy. As a result, the managers are often disposed to see themselves as pied pipers who choose corporate direction and policy, signal them clearly, and over time attract shareholders who like their tune. Those who disagree are always free to sell their shares.

Carried to its logical extreme, this approach defines the shareholders' interest as being identical with that of the professional manager. However, this mirror image splits when management faces the possibility of a takeover bid or corporate raid. More than any others, these challenges force corporate managers to focus on performance (and therefore goals) that might create disaffection among the shareholders. In addition, they test the managers' traditional identification with the company's loyal investors because the issues in question inevitably relate to choices that have the potential to affect near-term share values significantly, with little apparent concern for their long-term implications or sustainability.

How managers respond to actual takeover bids varies from case to case. Some change their policies and performances; others mount an active defense. The important issue here is not what they do, but how the possibility of such events affects their thinking under ordinary circumstances. Are incumbent managers powerfully and persistently reminded of investor priorities by the fact that they might someday lose control to a rival management team? Or does the shareholder constituency's influence rise and fall with specific market-related events including merger and acquisition cycles as well as takeovers and corporate raids? In our experience the latter description fits management's behavior more closely: once an immediate threat has passed, it tends to be business as usual.

On the basis of these observations some readers may conclude that professional management has both the power and the will to frustrate shareholders' legitimate objectives and interests. Most if not all managements would deny this vigorously—and believe what they say. However, as we have discovered, professional management's vision of the shareholder's true interest subordinates shareholder wealth to corporate wealth. Therefore its customary capital-market strategies are designed to protect and enhance the future corporate wealth on which the organization's survival depends, and it will be inclined to use all the means at its disposal to dilute or deflect alternative visions which conflict with its chosen path.

Strategies for Expanding Managerial Choice: The Product Market

Operating realities account for the strong influence product markets exercise over corporate goals. As we recall, these realities include:

- The extended time frame necessary to develop a stable, viable competitive position in major domestic and international product markets;

- Competitive, technological, financial, and psychological barriers to entry and exit;

- Management's competitive and psychological imperative to develop, hold, and—if possible—improve market shares;

- Corporate dependence on primary product markets for continuous funding of overhead costs;

- Major domestic and international competitors whose existence enforces consumers' demands for desired quantities of quality products at competitive prices.

Together these factors compel management to keep pace with the industry's growth rate; to invest whatever capital is required to support increased capacity and technological advances; and to provide goods and services at competitive prices and profit margins. Thus in the extreme case a one-product, one-market firm is wholly captive to its product-market environment, at least in the short run, because underlying economic and competitive variables define both the size and pace of its investments and their potential return.

Two strategies provide potential avenues of escape from the product market's discipline. One focuses on industry dominance, the other on diversification. Both were actively practiced at most of the companies included in this study.

Corporate managers' goals for their primary product market often included the exhortation to be Number One. These battle cries did not preclude an interest in careful market segmentation or proper positioning in the industry's most promising sectors. But it was commonly assumed that industry leadership provides major competitive advantages and that it frees management from the need to make knee jerk responses to rivals' initiatives. Product and price changes, marketing strategies, innovations in capacity and technology: all were thought to be firmly in the industry leaders' hands. In the best of all possible worlds a dominant position implies that the company leads the customer in matters of style, quality, volume, and price; while at a minimum it relieves management of much of the uncertainty facing an industry follower. Thus the leader's managers play a major role in setting industry direction, even though they cannot determine it completely.

Whether real or imagined, the advantages of being Number One were important to top managers as they sought to escape the product market's discipline. However, this leadership goal contained a potential trap set by the economics and competitive dynamics of the industry they sought to lead. Having fought and won many a battle en route to the top, management could arrive and find itself at the helm of a mature or declining industry, with modest growth prospects and inferior, or even nonsustaining, rates of return. Being the best would not be good enough in that case, unless the company had other significant product markets. If management had failed to provide alternatives to the industry it knew best, it would have won—and lost.

Recognizing the risks of the industry life cycle, most of the managements in the study tried to escape product-market dependency by diversifying. For the majority this entailed a strategy of constrained diversification: the search for new revenue streams in product markets where the company was believed to be uniquely competent and possess comparative advantage. These searches often lasted for several decades and proceeded slowly and intermittently. Periods of diversification were followed by periods of sorting-out and consolidation; while new long-term income streams, capable of complementing or replacing traditional product markets, emerged gradually and in their own time.

The advantage of achieving significant diversification is obvious: It greatly reduces any one product market's power to hold the company hostage to its economic conditions. In the extreme case a well-diversified company could walk away from its competitive position—or threaten to do so—without endangering corporate continuity or solvency. In reality few, if any, managements have this freedom. On the contrary, despite a decade of vigorous diversification activity, many of the study companies remained highly dependent on a few dominant product markets.

Table 8-1 contains a diversification index for each company in the research sample. The index has been calculated so that it reflects both the number of product markets in which the company was active and the proportion of corporate cash flows generated by each. Thus it takes into account the relative differences among product markets, so that truly undiversified companies (i.e., those in which one or two product markets supply virtually all the returns) will be accurately classified. The index ranges from a theoretical maximum of one, for a company engaged in ten product markets with sales equally divided among them, to a minimum of zero, for a one-product, one-market concern.[2]

The actual range of diversification among these large, mature corporations was wide. The index floor was set by Company A, whose management remained firmly committed to a one-industry identity, while the ceiling was set by Company L, one of two classified as a conglomerate because its management followed a strategy of unconstrained diversification. (The other conglomerate, Company I, changed little during this period.) As can be seen, five companies increased their level of diversity over the ten years, while three remained virtually the same and four became somewhat less diverse. Thus the index also counters the stereotypical view of diversification as a process of radical transformation. Overall the companies ended the period much as they had begun.

To pursue their diversification strategies many of these top managements had to set aside their preference for strict financial self-sufficiency. As the reader will recall, this was a central precept in the funding of *established* product markets; but it was not applied with equal rigor to new

Table 8-1. Diversification Indexes for Sample Companies, 1969–1978

Company	1978	1977	1976	1975	1974	1973	1972	1971	1970	1969
A	.123	.105	.114	.132	.131	.156	.166	.158	.172	.196
B	.226	.231	.221	.257*	.299	.308	.283	.243	.233	.225
C	.331	.340	.367	.381	.417	.384	.400	.394	.396	.400
D	.364	.363	.279	.274	.250	.246*	.203	.237	.248	.243
E	.404	.377	.365	.405	.409	.459	.475	.475	.472	.477
F	.426	.432	.435	.431	.414	.406	.399	.349	.266	.230
G	.475	.444	.474	.449	.441	.443	.419	.428	.410	.390
H	.512	.511	.495	.468	.457	.435	.401	.390	.365	.341
I	.573	.572	.560	.555	.590	.582	.572	.557	.553	.562
J	.578	.581	.583	.570	.577	.558	.559	.554	.575	.574
K	.593	.592*	.473	.476	.451	.440	.445	.450	.433	.426
L	.707	.706	.726	.724	.736	.740	.735	.747	.758	.766

Note. * indicates that the time series for the diversification index is discontinuous due to a change in classification of the lines of business. Appendix B contains a full explanation of the diversification index.

163

product-market initiatives. In particular, these managements often chose
to fund acquisitions through an exchange of stock, a decision which was
partly deliberate and partly in response to the acquired businesses' preference for stock rather than cash.

The effect of these funding decisions on the company's capital accounts can be illustrated by plotting the percentage increase in the firm's
outstanding common stock (based on dollar book value) against its diver-

Figure 8:1   Company A: Record of Product Market Diversification, 1969-78

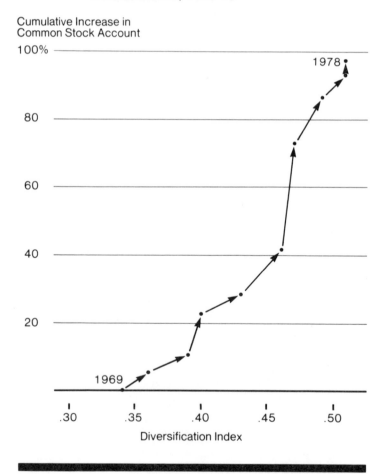

Cumulative Increase in
Common Stock Account

Diversification Index

sification index. Figures 8-1–8-3 present such graphs for three study companies, all engaged in diversifying through acquisition. As is readily apparent, each management felt the need to depart from strict self-sufficiency to fund the firm's entry into new product markets.[3]

During the ten-year period plotted, Company A's diversification index rose steadily from .34 to .51 as its management made a large number

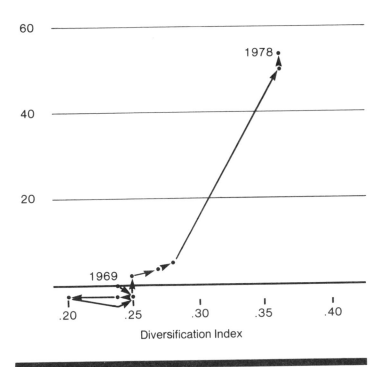

Figure 8:2   Company B: Record of Product Market Diversification, 1969-78

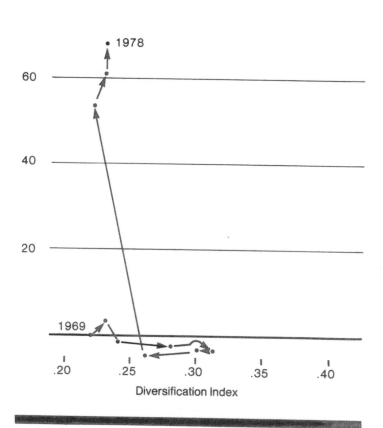

Figure 8:3 Company C: Record of Product Market Diversification, 1969-78

of acquisitions (Figure 8-1). However, as its capital stock account increased by 96 percent at the same time, the price of those acquisitions seemed to be a substantial dilution in the original shareholders' equity. In fact this was not the entire picture. Retained earnings increased 335 percent during the same period, and the common stock account represented only 22 percent of the total common-equity book value in 1978. In addition, the stock's market value increased by a greater factor than its book value, thereby indicating that the owners' aggregate market value remained intact.

Figure 8-2 shows Company B's diversification record for the same ten-year period. Initially the company changed little, as we see, and the small shifts in its index reflected slight product-market variations. However, the company began to move quite rapidly after 1974, with the help of a few very important acquisitions. In the process its capital stock increased by 53 percent, while its diversification index rose to .36.

The failure of Company C's acquisition strategy stands in sharp contrast to the other companies' successes. As Figure 8-3 indicates, the company raised its diversification index significantly from .22 to .31, only to fall back to .22 in 1978. Thus it showed signs of returning to the high degree of concentration typical of its earlier years, with only modest shifts in the corporate earnings base to offset the 67 percent increase in the capital stock account. In essence management had sacrificed true self-sufficiency without materially improving the company diversity.

For companies able to maintain or achieve significantly higher diversification the strategy promised greater independence from each individual product market's competitive demands. However, other dimensions of the financial goals system paid the price for this freedom. Most obvious, perhaps, was the greater sensitivity to capital-market concerns and priorities inevitably required when diversification was achieved through external acquisitions involving substantial amounts of new equity. An aggressive diversification strategy could not be pursued without the capital-market constituency's cooperation and approval, as reflected in rising stock prices and a strong and rising price-earnings ratio. Thus the company had to be doing the things that all its investors would like—including the professionals who made the market for the company's shares.

A second potential cost reflected the fact that as a company became more diversified, its overall performance became more average because of the market basket of businesses it included. Obviously every management sought to acquire new product markets with high, sustained rates of growth and above-average returns. But these results were not always fulfilled, and mistakes were not easily shed. Consequently, at any point in time, most companies had a range of performers, including some that were second rate. To the extent that the good performers supported and funded the bad the internal capital market was doing its work. But overall corporate results did not always reflect management's goals and expectations for the company as a whole.

Finally—and ironically—management had to reckon with the effect of the company's new-found product-market constituents on its goals. Diversification might reduce the company's vulnerability to the competitive forces of its traditional product line; but at the divisional level the name of the game remained market share in each product market in which the firm competed. Consequently, product-market forces tended to reassert themselves once management had achieved the desired degree of diversity, or events imposed a period of consolidation on the company. Industry trends again paced corporate investment, and product-market priorities reappeared as the company settled into its new product-market configuration.

Strategies for Expanding Managerial Choice: The Organizational Constituency

Because the CEO and the other top managers are members of the organization, yet must act independently of it at times, their relations with this constituency are the most ambiguous and complex of all. Further complications are created by the fact that they may interact continuously in many ways. Strategy, practice, and behavior all send important messages, while communications range from explicit formal documents to subtle looks, phrases, and gestures. Finally, even though this study treats the organizational constituency as one uniform body for reasons of simplicity and clarity, it actually contains many competing subgroups with diverse points of view.

Nevertheless, these groups share certain fundamental interests with the career professional managers who lead the organization. Among them are the superordinate goals that constitute the core of the formal and informal goals system: the commitment to survival, independence, self-sufficiency, and individual opportunity. The most obvious and persistent manifestation of these goals appears in the quest for continuous profitable growth. As previously noted, such growth is considered an essential foundation for the job security, opportunity, upward mobility, and financial reward which attract and hold superior managers and staff personnel.

To the extent that top management separates itself from this organizational agenda, several considerations enter in. Prominent among them is the likelihood that at certain times the organization may be fixed on goals that no longer seem relevant to those in charge. The word leadership clearly implies a vision of the organization's future significantly in advance of, or different from, the past or the present. However, as manifest in new statements of business mission or corporate and financial goals, such visions can signal changes that the existing organization may dislike or even actively resist. Thus top management may need the elbow room provided by the firm's real—or perceived—opportunities to trade off the organization's priorities against its own, without measurably sacrificing employees' commitment or loyalty.

Individual CEOs and their immediate subordinates also tend to identify with one or another constituent's priorities. In many instances these sympathies are tactical, the result of a deliberate strategy in which top management leans one way or the other to promote its view of the corporation's long-term interest. For example, the managers may come down hard on stockholder issues to emphasize a near-term priority for profitability and resources at the expense of growth; or, conversely, a deep and lasting commitment to established product markets may be asserted simply in acknowledgment of limited alternatives and comparative advantage. However, it is also true that some CEOs are philosophically drawn to one particular constituency because its priorities accord with their own concept of private enterprise. In these instances the company's constituencies have a preestablished order, which exists apart from the exigencies of any given set of circumstances.

Because of these factors, as well as their responsibility for effecting a working balance among competing constituent interests, top managers typically try to maintain an independent perspective, distinct from established organizational expectations. To this end they draw on a variety of means including: intervention in resource-allocation decisions; the proclamation of new corporate goals, strategies, and business missions; the selection and promotion of subordinates (including a CEO's choice of successor); board appointments which reflect their preference for active (or passive), internal (or external) members; and control of the form and distribution of organizational rewards.

Diversification decisions illustrate the tension between corporate leadership and organizational priorities well, because the members of the existing organization are likely to be highly ambivalent about the benefits. On the one hand, they tend to recognize that the company's growth and opportunities can only be sustained by developing new income streams to replace mature established product markets. On the other, they know that the new product markets will inevitably become strong competitors for corporate resources and potential power bases for rival top-management candidates. Thus aggressive leadership is typically required to stake out a radical change in the company's direction; and top management must use all its official and persuasive powers to overcome the inertia of the status quo.

Extended observation of corporate leadership indicates that top management commonly uses its power to modulate constituent interests so that no one predominates continuously. Although these modulations could reflect a lack of clearcut priorities, it is much more likely that they represent a realistic response to organizational life. Large and complex human organizations cannot fully attend to more than a few goals at a time. Other important priorities are inevitably distorted, therefore, and ultimately must be corrected. Growth and return on investment, consolidation and diversification, building and deploying resources, short-term performance and long-term potential—these classic pendulum swings illustrate this process well. Wise management recognizes an excess of zeal applied to one or another worthy objective and initiates a counterbalancing response. If it is successful, the entire corporate enterprise moves forward at an orderly pace.

The Limits of Managerial Independence

The top managements of modern American industrial corporations have considerable discretion and power over large aggregations of wealth they do not own, markets they do not dominate, employees they do not control, and a society which could potentially rise up and deprive them of their power through its legislative, executive, and judicial authority. CEOs and their teams can commit large sums to risky investments at home and abroad and walk away, apparently unscathed, from subsequent losses. They can create heavy debt obligations or none at all, expand the stockholders' share of earnings or diminish it, issue large blocks of ownership or repurchase those already in existence. Operations deemed unprofitable or incompatible can be shut down on their orders, and resources can be reallocated across a wide range of corporate activities. Even critical technological advances are within their control through their ability to focus and fund R&D, time new productive capacity, and target new product-market developments or acquisitions.

Given these facts (and a business press continually filled with fresh examples of American management's freedom), it may seem contradictory to speak, as we have, about constituency control of the corporate financial goals system and management's need for deliberate sustained strategies and practices to relax that discipline. Apparently these strategies are remarkably successful in the longer run. In fact, they are. Case histories from this study and general observation provide many examples of management's strategic success across the entire spectrum of constituency power. To consider the capital market first, managements carried out active growth strategies for decades without requesting a single dollar of new cash from their shareholders and only conservative amounts from their lenders. Thus they have implemented a strategy of financial self-sufficiency with the shareholders' tacit approval and without any evidence of active or passive resistance. Further, they have been able to operate for extended periods with considerable slack in the financial, economic, and human resources under their direct control. In part this has been due to the complexity of the corporate system, which often hides existing slack from insiders as well as outsiders. But even substantial amounts of liquid reserves, highlighted in the published balance sheets, can persist for extended periods unassaulted from without or within.

Over time many managements have effected radical changes in their corporate and investment strategies. In the process they have also effected equally radical transformations in the composition of the shareholder group. Conservative, income-oriented, long-term investors have given way to aggressive, capital gains-oriented, short-term investors (and vice versa), as management shifted from mature, low-growth, low-risk strategies to nascent, high-growth, high-risk strategies (or the reverse). For the most part those who recognized the change and were uncomfortable with it sold out quickly and invested elsewhere; while those who tried to arouse the shareholders to resist management rarely met with success. (Given incumbent management's power to mount a vigorous counter-offensive, the frequent failure of such efforts should not be surprising.)

Managements' efforts to diminish the product-market constituency's power through market dominance and diversification have often been similarly successful. As we have seen, a number of companies achieved substantial diversity in their portfolios of major product markets and in the distribution of earnings among them within a decade or less. As a result the dictates of the competitive forces in each product market were significantly reduced on critical issues of corporate survival and continuity. Management could approach marginal investment decisions more objectively and say no when it was persuaded that better alternatives existed.

Evidence of absolute market dominance is harder to find. As far as could be seen, no single company was absolutely Number One in its particular product markets. However, a major market share protected by significant entry barriers could be almost as efficacious. By giving management significant control over events, such positions reduced uncertainty and improved flexibility. Moreover, they could be sustained over long periods of time—and were.

In terms of top management's organizational strategies the best evidence of success comes from employment data. At many of the companies studied there was considerable stability among key corporate management personnel, particularly over the tenure of any one chief executive. Thus it seems fair to conclude that these top executives were reasonably successful in building and maintaining strong, loyal, and dedicated work forces and in insulating their firms from the potentially disruptive forces of the external human resource market.

Does this evidence mean that given the will, the time, and the opportunity top management can ignore its key constituents' priorities, overcome the constraints on its choices, and set corporate goals and direction with perfect independence? On balance we think not; and, although the evidence for this conclusion is necessarily subjective and judgmental, it can be placed in the context of the more objective data developed in the preceding chapters.

Capital market forces take their most specific form in the debt and earnings-retention policies which together determine the slope of a company's self-sufficient growth line. Over time management may be able to tilt this line up or down, by reconstituting the shareholder and lender groups, so that different risk and reinvestment preferences prevail. And, in this process, it will produce a greater or lesser growth potential for any given return on investment and thereby gain greater discretionary power over these parts of the goals system.

However, there will always be some absolute limit to the risk lenders are willing to assume before asserting control, just as there will always be some limit to the earnings shareholders are willing to reinvest. (In the extreme case, where the limit is *all* the current earnings, the potential rate of growth will equal the rate of return.) Moreover, management cannot set its funding policies in isolation. At the least it must consider its key competitors' strategies as it chooses its own debt and dividend levels.

Comparable qualifications hedge top management's freedom to operate a company for an extended period at growth and rate of return levels that place it above or below the line of self-sufficiency. Corporate managers do follow such courses, as we have seen, either as part of a deliberate strategy or because of events beyond their control. But in so doing they run the risk that their companies will be seriously over- or underfunded and therefore particularly vulnerable to capital-market forces. Serious and sustained underfunding increases the likelihood that the company will have to call on the external capital market for a major infusion of new money, while serious and sustained overfunding feeds the interest of corporate raiders. Thus management is likely to show increased sensitivity to capital-market expectations in either case.

In fact, some degree of capital-market sensitivity is always essential, however much it waxes or wanes with events. Actual corporate experiences over time produce rates of growth that oscillate in a wide band above and below the ideal level for self-sustained funding, and management is often unable—or unwilling—to dampen these swings. Therefore it must be mindful of the external capital market's role as a contingency reserve and as a potential challenger for control. Whatever changes management can induce in the composition of this constituency it will always have some market presence to reckon with.

A comparable relationship exists with the product-market constituency because every company is subject to the competitive pressures of the product markets in which it seeks to protect or achieve a leadership role. Management can radically transform its company by relocating its operations and earnings from one industry to another. It can move from one dominant interrelated set of product markets to another over time. It can even acquire a highly diversified earnings base spread out over several unrelated industries and thereby become permanently less vulnerable to any one industry's competitive demands. But whatever the company's degree of diversification, it must keep pace with industry growth, product innovation, technology, and productive capacity, and it must seek a quality product at a competitive price. Thus top management must remain responsive to the product market's pressures and its priorities for investment and competitive return. In reality a diversified company's management escapes the discipline of one industry only to find itself the captive of another—or of many.

A similar paradox characterizes top management's relationship with its organization. This is so because the conditions that attract superior management and staff—growth, innovation, change, leadership, and re-ward—must be perpetuated to retain them. If top management success-fully builds a uniquely attractive corporate image and provides career identities for talented, highly motivated employees, it derives considera-ble freedom from the job inertia such an environment creates. However, it cannot trade off its organization's goals indefinitely, without running the risk of losing its edge in the most critical area: the quality of its human resources.

For these reasons we conclude that top management can never wholly free itself from its constituents' priorities or the constraints these priorities impose. Given the will and the ability, management can trans-form its entire constituency base and thereby redefine each element of the financial goals system to maximize its discretionary power. But be-cause the enterprise requires the resources those constituencies supply, top management cannot do away with the goals system itself or the trade-offs the system mandates. Management can choose its partners in the markets for funds, human resources, and products; but it will always have some partners to accommodate to ensure corporate survival.

A Broader Perspective

This study was premised on the principle that we must understand the business world as it is before we can think sensibly about what it ought to be. Therefore our observations have been presented as clearly and objectively as possible, with a minimum of editorial comment. No study is totally free of research bias, of course, but conscious efforts have been made to avoid judgments about the economic and social utility of the organizational and managerial behavior described. Now the follow-ing comments are in order.

Having shared the facts, it is time for a few personal observations. In the course of this study it became apparent that the paramount impor-tance attached to organizational survival by individual managers con-trasts sharply with the views of those interested in the management of the economy as a whole. From the latter perspective the economic or social value of a marginal firm approaches zero and in any case cannot be mea-sured by the self-interest of its managers. However, individual manager's priorities are understandable (given that survival instincts are natural and inevitable for individuals and groups alike) and may have social validity as well, if we grant that organizational capacity has social value.

There can be little question that the capacity to organize and manage large aggregations of value-creating work is a scarce national resource, which typically takes a long time to develop and a short time to destroy. Moreover, the ability to produce efficiently and compete effectively in large-scale economic activities depends on the existence of such organizational units. Therefore, it is both natural and desirable that the leaders of these organizations use all the legal and ethical means at their disposal to preserve their own unique social function. May the best person win.

Individual managers' desire for independence can be justified along similar lines, because the opportunity to run an enterprise on one's own authority motivates—and rewards—the best business leadership. What we have called discretionary space contributes greatly to organizational efficiency, therefore, as do the attitudes and strategies that legitimize an independent managerial perspective. As has been noted, corporate leaders regard the idea that they are anyone's agents with anathema, and they are firmly committed to self-sufficiency as a prerequisite for the independent course essential in a real-world school of hard knocks.

When we turn from the individual to the organization, the question of survival becomes more complex. If top management anticipates the permanent deterioration of its immediate industry base and sees only financial decline or insolvency associated with a continuing industry role, should it aspire to corporate immortality and a life beyond the death of the industry? The current debate over the legitimate bounds of corporate diversification suggests that some would answer no. They would argue that loyalty is better than flight—even if it means going down with the industry ship.

Most top managers do not share this view. On the contrary, the study clearly reveals management's deep and abiding instinct for organizational survival beyond the decline of any individual earnings base. Further, it indicates that top managers recognize the need to anticipate this deterioration before it becomes well-advanced, so that resources can be repositioned with minimal losses in value and momentum. Given the uncertainty of these events, some managements may jump ship prematurely or mistakenly or choose vessels less seaworthy than those they abandoned. But the critical issue here is less the managers' final scorecards than the social utility of their common view. Once again a judgment should be made about the importance of organizational survival.

In our perception the best of these large, complex organizations do represent critical national resources, which should not be discarded casually. Therefore, we would support the right of individual managements to define comparative advantage broadly and perpetuate it in whatever industrial environment proves hospitable. This is not an argument for bigness per se, nor for public life-support systems for ailing giants; rather, it is an argument for allowing such organizations to seek out legitimate fresh opportunities.

A second set of concerns associated with managerial independence focuses on the abuses of power. These concerns inevitably arise in response to the prospect of a few, powerful corporate leaders endowed with wide discretionary power and the right (and ability) to perpetuate it, and they are legitimate. Evidence of the misuse of power is regularly brought before the public, and nothing stated herein should be taken as arguing that the system works perfectly or that the potential for abuses does not exist.

However, the evidence of this study strongly suggests that most top managers are significantly constrained by the internal and external checks and balances of the goals system. In some cases a long-term view must be taken to see the discipline at work. But, in general, top managements are not free to ignore the things that matter most to their varying constituencies. On the contrary, they recognize the need to effect a workable balance among their constituents' priorities and their own; they acknowledge their responsibility to those constituents in formulating corporate policy; and they are sensitive to the fact that their control can be challenged from within and without, and that existing mechanisms could deprive them of their power. Last, but not least, their funds-flow decisions are necessarily constrained by the tangible and objective discipline of the goals system, which reinforces critical constituent demands.

The primacy of this economic discipline reinforces another of the study's findings, namely, the absence of social responsibility as a significant factor in management's corporate goals. When this study was in its planning stages during the late 1970s, we did not expect to reach such a conclusion. The period was marked by widespread consumer and social activism, and there seemed to be a growing corporate awareness of social issues, particularly among the chief executives of major corporations, who were fond of citing the extent to which these issues occupied their time in Washington and elsewhere. Consequently, we expected to find evidence of this growing social conscience reflected in corporate goals. In fact, extensive and close observation indicates that this perception was a veneer. Beneath the surface, where the hard decisions were being made, it was still very much business as usual.

This is not intended as a negative or cynical comment. Our documents and interviews provide abundant evidence that most managers honestly believe in the real social value added by their work. However, that added value is *economic* value, and the discipline apparent in the financial goals and resource-allocation system is an economic discipline, pure and simple, run according to economic laws in economic markets. Corporations may function as instruments of social change at times; but they are not seen in that light by their managers. To the extent that society intervenes effectively in corporate activity, it does so through the competitive discipline of the markets in which a firm functions, rather than through moral suasion or confrontation. At times, of course, society also acts through legislation and regulation; but these are usually blunt instruments of last resort. Its greatest power to limit abuses and reinforce responsible management lies in the effectiveness of the competitive discipline of the markets from which the firm draws its critical resources.

One last comment before concluding. The relevance of the financial goals system is not limited to private enterprises run on profit-making lines. Its basic structure is applicable to any organization that has a responsibility to manage scarce financial and human resources for a defined social purpose. In practice it applies equally well to not-for-profit organizations, such as mutual insurance companies and hospitals, to state-owned enterprises such as rail systems and post offices, and even to the industry of socialized societies. Each of these enterprises has an implicit or explicit business mission which requires continuing investment of funds. If its mission is central to an important social need, the enterprise is likely to be growing more or less continuously. In that case it will have a group of career employees and managers who identify with and benefit from its growth and continuity. It will have inflows of funds, related to the price of its goods or services, that must cover costs and provide a surplus or profit to support its growth. It is even likely to have funds transfers of one sort or another, which are the counterparts of the private corporation's equity and debt flows. These flows must be in balance and they must fund the needed growth. The organization may not be self-sustaining—in which case its customers, communities, or society at large must make up the deficit, or it will fail. But its organizational and financial goals must function to keep the system in balance, if it is to succeed in the long run. Thus not-for-profit and profit-making companies ultimately meet in a common concern for the survival of their economic and social missions. In the final analysis the difference is not how the financial system works, or even who owns it, but rather who controls it, and with what goals in mind.

Notes

1. Gordon Donaldson, *Strategy for Financial Mobility* (Boston: Division of Research, Harvard Graduate School of Business Administration, 1969).

2. Appendix A contains a detailed explanation of the diversification index.

3. It is important to note that the figures used included *all* changes in the common stock, including shares issued under stock options, stock purchase plans, and new issues for cash, reduced by shares brought into treasury. Shares issued in exchange for acquired companies could have been broken out, but this information would have made it materially easier to identify the companies concerned.

Appendix A

Tables of Self-Sustaining Growth

Tables A-1 through A-4 were generated from a simple computer program based on the self-sustaining growth equation found in Chapter 4. They provide a practical illustration for managers who wish to examine in detail the tradeoff between growth and return on investment in their own company. By using their own corporate data (including the appropriate after-tax cost of debt), managers can produce equivalent tables for their companies.

Note that these tables are intended to provide an *approximate* measure of the sustainable growth rate which can be attained for any given rate of return on investment (RONA). The growth rates indicated are growth rates of Net Assets, but they can be taken as an indication of attainable growth rates of Sales if the ratio of Sales to Net Assets remains reasonably stable over time.

The tables can also be reproduced from the computer program in graphic form as illustrated in Figures A-1 and A-2. The graphics provide a clear visual impression of the relative leverage provided by earnings retention and debt for higher sustainable growth rates for any given RONA.

Table A-1. Earnings Retention Rate = 1.00; After-Tax Interest Rate = 0.05

Implicit Growth Rate	Debt/Equity Ratio										
	0.00	0.10	0.20	0.30	0.40	0.50	0.60	0.70	0.80	0.90	1.00
0.00	0.000	−0.005	−0.010	−0.015	−0.020	−0.025	−0.030	−0.035	−0.040	−0.045	−0.050
0.01	0.010	0.006	0.002	−0.002	−0.006	−0.010	−0.014	−0.018	−0.022	−0.026	−0.030
0.02	0.020	0.017	0.014	0.011	0.008	0.005	0.002	−0.001	−0.004	−0.007	−0.010
0.03	0.030	0.028	0.026	0.024	0.022	0.020	0.018	0.016	0.014	0.012	0.010
0.04	0.040	0.039	0.038	0.037	0.036	0.035	0.034	0.033	0.032	0.031	0.030
0.05	0.050	0.050	0.050	0.050	0.050	0.050	0.050	0.050	0.050	0.050	0.050
0.06	0.060	0.061	0.062	0.063	0.064	0.065	0.066	0.067	0.068	0.069	0.070
0.07	0.070	0.072	0.074	0.076	0.078	0.080	0.082	0.084	0.086	0.088	0.090
0.08	0.080	0.083	0.086	0.089	0.092	0.095	0.098	0.101	0.104	0.107	0.110
0.09	0.090	0.094	0.098	0.102	0.106	0.110	0.114	0.118	0.122	0.126	0.130
0.10	0.100	0.105	0.110	0.115	0.120	0.125	0.130	0.135	0.140	0.145	0.150
0.11	0.110	0.116	0.122	0.128	0.134	0.140	0.146	0.152	0.158	0.164	0.170
0.12	0.120	0.127	0.134	0.141	0.148	0.155	0.162	0.169	0.176	0.183	0.190
0.13	0.130	0.138	0.146	0.154	0.162	0.170	0.178	0.186	0.194	0.202	0.210
0.14	0.140	0.149	0.158	0.167	0.176	0.185	0.194	0.203	0.212	0.221	0.230
0.15	0.150	0.160	0.170	0.180	0.190	0.200	0.210	0.220	0.230	0.240	0.250
0.16	0.160	0.171	0.182	0.193	0.204	0.215	0.226	0.237	0.248	0.259	0.270
0.17	0.170	0.182	0.194	0.206	0.218	0.230	0.242	0.254	0.266	0.278	0.290
0.18	0.180	0.193	0.206	0.219	0.232	0.245	0.258	0.271	0.284	0.297	0.310
0.19	0.190	0.204	0.218	0.232	0.246	0.260	0.274	0.288	0.302	0.316	0.330
0.20	0.200	0.215	0.230	0.245	0.260	0.275	0.290	0.305	0.320	0.335	0.350

R O N A

Table A-2. Earnings Retention Rate = 0.75; After-Tax Interest Rate = 0.05

Implicit Growth Rate	Debt/Equity Ratio										
	0.00	0.10	0.20	0.30	0.40	0.50	0.60	0.70	0.80	0.90	1.00
0.00	0.000	− 0.004	− 0.008	− 0.011	− 0.015	− 0.019	− 0.023	− 0.026	− 0.030	− 0.034	− 0.038
0.01	0.008	0.005	0.001	− 0.002	− 0.005	− 0.008	− 0.011	− 0.014	− 0.017	− 0.020	− 0.023
0.02	0.015	0.013	0.011	0.008	0.006	0.004	0.001	− 0.001	− 0.003	− 0.005	− 0.008
0.03	0.023	0.021	0.020	0.018	0.017	0.015	0.014	0.012	0.011	0.009	0.008
0.04	0.030	0.029	0.029	0.028	0.027	0.026	0.026	0.025	0.024	0.023	0.023
0.05	0.038	0.038	0.038	0.038	0.038	0.038	0.038	0.038	0.038	0.038	0.038
0.06	0.045	0.046	0.047	0.047	0.048	0.049	0.050	0.050	0.051	0.052	0.053
0.07	0.053	0.054	0.056	0.057	0.059	0.060	0.062	0.063	0.065	0.066	0.068
0.08	0.060	0.062	0.065	0.067	0.069	0.071	0.074	0.076	0.078	0.080	0.083
0.09	0.068	0.071	0.074	0.077	0.080	0.083	0.086	0.089	0.092	0.095	0.098
0.10	0.075	0.079	0.083	0.086	0.090	0.094	0.098	0.101	0.105	0.109	0.113
0.11	0.083	0.087	0.091	0.096	0.101	0.105	0.110	0.114	0.118	0.123	0.127
0.12	0.090	0.095	0.100	0.106	0.111	0.116	0.121	0.127	0.132	0.137	0.142
0.13	0.098	0.103	0.109	0.115	0.121	0.127	0.134	0.140	0.145	0.151	0.158
0.14	0.105	0.112	0.119	0.125	0.132	0.139	0.146	0.152	0.159	0.166	0.173
0.15	0.113	0.120	0.128	0.135	0.143	0.150	0.158	0.165	0.173	0.180	0.188
0.16	0.120	0.128	0.137	0.145	0.153	0.161	0.170	0.178	0.186	0.194	0.203
0.17	0.128	0.137	0.146	0.155	0.164	0.173	0.182	0.191	0.200	0.209	0.218
0.18	0.135	0.145	0.155	0.164	0.174	0.184	0.194	0.203	0.213	0.223	0.233
0.19	0.143	0.153	0.164	0.174	0.185	0.195	0.206	0.216	0.227	0.237	0.248
0.20	0.150	0.161	0.173	0.184	0.195	0.206	0.218	0.229	0.240	0.251	0.263

R O N A

Table A-3. Earnings Retention Rate = 0.50; After-Tax Interest Rate = 0.05

Implicit Growth Rate	Debt/Equity Ratio										
	0.00	0.10	0.20	0.30	0.40	0.50	0.60	0.70	0.80	0.90	1.00
0.00	0.000	-0.003	-0.005	-0.008	-0.010	-0.013	-0.015	-0.018	-0.020	-0.023	-0.025
0.01	0.005	0.003	0.001	-0.001	-0.003	-0.005	-0.007	-0.009	-0.011	-0.013	-0.015
0.02	0.010	0.009	0.007	0.005	0.004	0.002	0.001	-0.001	-0.002	-0.004	-0.005
0.03	0.015	0.014	0.013	0.012	0.011	0.010	0.009	0.008	0.007	0.006	0.005
0.04	0.020	0.020	0.019	0.019	0.018	0.018	0.017	0.017	0.016	0.016	0.015
0.05	0.025	0.025	0.025	0.025	0.025	0.025	0.025	0.025	0.025	0.025	0.025
0.06	0.030	0.031	0.031	0.032	0.032	0.033	0.033	0.034	0.034	0.035	0.035
0.07	0.035	0.036	0.037	0.038	0.039	0.040	0.041	0.042	0.043	0.044	0.045
0.08	0.040	0.042	0.043	0.045	0.046	0.048	0.049	0.051	0.052	0.054	0.055
0.09	0.045	0.047	0.049	0.051	0.053	0.055	0.057	0.059	0.061	0.063	0.065
0.10	0.050	0.053	0.055	0.058	0.060	0.063	0.065	0.068	0.070	0.073	0.075
0.11	0.055	0.058	0.061	0.064	0.067	0.070	0.073	0.076	0.079	0.082	0.085
0.12	0.060	0.063	0.067	0.071	0.074	0.077	0.081	0.085	0.088	0.091	0.095
0.13	0.065	0.069	0.073	0.077	0.081	0.085	0.089	0.093	0.097	0.101	0.105
0.14	0.070	0.075	0.079	0.084	0.088	0.093	0.097	0.102	0.106	0.111	0.115
0.15	0.075	0.080	0.085	0.090	0.095	0.100	0.105	0.110	0.115	0.120	0.125
0.16	0.080	0.086	0.091	0.097	0.102	0.108	0.113	0.119	0.124	0.130	0.135
0.17	0.085	0.091	0.097	0.103	0.109	0.115	0.121	0.127	0.133	0.139	0.145
0.18	0.090	0.097	0.103	0.110	0.116	0.123	0.129	0.136	0.142	0.149	0.155
0.19	0.095	0.102	0.109	0.116	0.123	0.130	0.137	0.144	0.151	0.158	0.165
0.20	0.100	0.108	0.115	0.123	0.130	0.138	0.145	0.153	0.160	0.168	0.175

RONA

Table A-4. Earnings Retention Rate = 0.25; After-Tax Interest Rate = 0.05

Implicit Growth Rate	Debt/Equity Ratio										
	0.00	0.10	0.20	0.30	0.40	0.50	0.60	0.70	0.80	0.90	1.00
0.00	0.000	−0.001	−0.003	−0.004	−0.005	−0.006	−0.008	−0.009	−0.010	−0.011	−0.013
0.01	0.003	0.002	.000	−0.001	−0.002	−0.003	−0.004	−0.005	−0.006	−0.007	−0.008
0.02	0.005	0.004	0.004	0.003	0.002	0.001	.000	.000	−0.001	−0.002	−0.003
0.03	0.008	0.007	0.007	0.006	0.006	0.005	0.005	0.004	0.004	0.003	0.003
0.04	0.010	0.010	0.010	0.009	0.009	0.009	0.009	0.008	0.008	0.008	0.008
0.05	0.013	0.013	0.013	0.013	0.013	0.013	0.013	0.013	0.013	0.013	0.013
0.06	0.015	0.015	0.016	0.016	0.016	0.016	0.017	0.017	0.017	0.017	0.018
0.07	0.018	0.018	0.019	0.019	0.020	0.020	0.021	0.021	0.022	0.022	0.023
0.08	0.020	0.021	0.022	0.022	0.023	0.024	0.025	0.025	0.026	0.027	0.028
0.09	0.023	0.024	0.025	0.026	0.027	0.028	0.029	0.030	0.031	0.032	0.033
0.10	0.025	0.026	0.028	0.029	0.030	0.031	0.033	0.034	0.035	0.036	0.038
0.11	0.028	0.029	0.030	0.032	0.034	0.035	0.037	0.038	0.040	0.041	0.043
0.12	0.030	0.032	0.034	0.035	0.037	0.039	0.041	0.042	0.044	0.046	0.048
0.13	0.033	0.035	0.036	0.038	0.041	0.043	0.044	0.046	0.048	0.050	0.052
0.14	0.035	0.037	0.040	0.042	0.044	0.046	0.049	0.051	0.053	0.055	0.058
0.15	0.038	0.040	0.043	0.045	0.048	0.050	0.053	0.055	0.058	0.060	0.063
0.16	0.040	0.043	0.046	0.048	0.051	0.054	0.057	0.059	0.062	0.065	0.068
0.17	0.043	0.046	0.049	0.052	0.055	0.058	0.061	0.064	0.067	0.070	0.073
0.18	0.045	0.048	0.052	0.055	0.058	0.061	0.065	0.068	0.071	0.074	0.078
0.19	0.048	0.051	0.055	0.058	0.062	0.065	0.069	0.072	0.076	0.079	0.083
0.20	0.050	0.054	0.058	0.061	0.065	0.069	0.073	0.076	0.080	0.084	0.088

R O N A

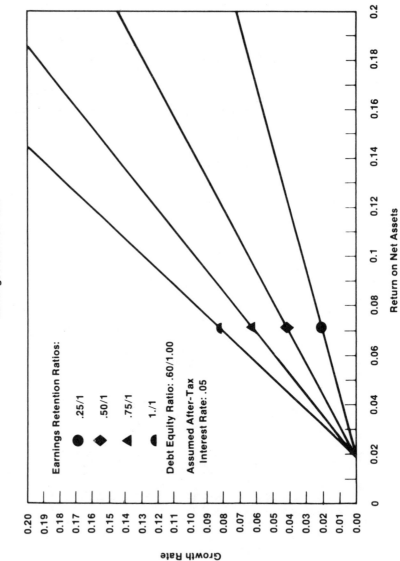

Figure A-1
Self Sustaining Growth: The Impact of Variations in the
Earnings Retention Rate

Figure A-2

Self Sustaining Growth: The Impact of Variations in the
Debt Equity Ratio

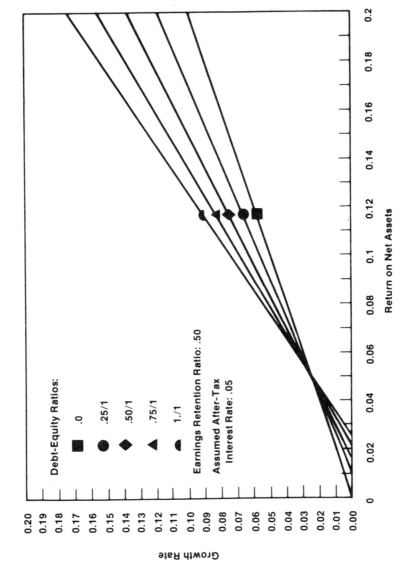

Appendix B
The Diversification Index

A complete index of diversification should be sensitive to at least two aspects of diversification: (1) The *number* of different markets in which the firm is engaged; and (2) the *distribution* of its cash flows or productive activity among those markets.

Traditionally used methods have been inadequate to capture these two dimensions of diversification. Counting product lines addresses the first dimension but not the second. The ratio of a company's sales in its primary market to its total sales partially measures the distribution of the company's cash flows (as between primary and secondary markets), but it neglects the number of different markets in which the firm is involved. A "compromise" solution—measuring the concentration of activity in the firm's two or three largest product markets—partially measures both the number and the relative dominance of the firm's major activities. However, this solution is unsatisfactory in that firms that differ greatly in their degree of diversification could have identical indices of unity. (For example, a single-product firm and a dual-product firm could generate the same index, despite differences in their actual degree of diversification.)

The index we have devised addresses these problems. It is defined by the formula:

$$D = -\log \sum_{i=1}^{n} s_i^2$$

where: n equals the total number of different product markets in which the firm is engaged; Σ equals a sum over all n product markets; and s_i equals the proportion of a firm's total dollar sales accounted for by the ith product market. The index takes a value of zero for a single-product market (i.e., no diversity whatsoever) and may, in principle, increase indefinitely thereafter, depending on the number and size distribution of a

This appendix was prepared by W. Carl Kester, Assistant Professor at the Harvard Business School. It is reprinted with changes from Donaldson and Lorsch, *Decision Making at the Top* (New York: Basic Books, 1983), pp. 178–80, by permission of the author and publisher.

firm's product markets. As a practical matter, however, it would be unusual to see the index rise much above 1.0. (To give a specific example, a company in ten different product markets, with sales divided equally among all ten markets, would have a diversification index value of one.)

This diversification index is a variant of an index of industrial concentration originally developed by Orris C. Herfindahl.[1] For our purposes the important part of the index is the term Σ_i^2. This term represents a weighting scheme for a firm's proportions of sales by product markets, where the weights are simply the fractions of sales themselves. The log transformation is employed for statistical reasons and in no way changes the ordinal ranking of levels of diversification derived simply from Σ_i^2.[2]

The index is sensitive to the *number* of activities in which the company is engaged because we sum over *all* of the firm's fraction of sales by product market. The index is also sensitive to the *distribution* of sales among product markets because each sales fraction squared is the proportion of total sales accounted for by a corresponding product market. Finally, by taking squares of each fraction of total sales, we ensure that our sum will never equal unity except in the case of a single-product company. Thus we avoid having an identical value of the index for firms with truly different degrees of diversification.

The Data

The data used to construct the diversification index were the company's reported sales by major product line. Several caveats should be mentioned in connection with the use of sales data of this type. First, the use of sales data obscures the fact that a company's actual cash flow from a particular product market may be quite different from its fraction of total cash flow (i.e., cash flow from a market can be negative, but sales cannot be). Thus an index constructed on the basis of sales data may belie the actual success of a company's diversification program. Second, the use of sales data renders the index sensitive to exogenous forces beyond management's control that change the composition of sales despite their consistent allocation of productive assets to each line of business. Thus changes in the index over time cannot wholly be ascribed to management's diversification goals. Third, comparability between firms is impaired to the extent that they vary in the detail with which they report sales by line of business.

Despite such drawbacks, reasons of convenience and availability dictated the use of sales by product line. Except in very recent years, assets by product line were usually not reported, and companies never compiled such data themselves until new federal reporting requirements forced them to do so. For better or worse, therefore, sales by product line are the data available over a useful length of time.

Notes

1. Orris C. Herfindahl, "Concentration in the U.S. Steel Industry" (DBA dissertation, Columbia University, 1950).

2. In *Industrial Market Structures and Economic Performance* (Chicago, IL: Rand McNally, 1970), p. 52, Frederick M. Scherer has pointed out that a statistical peculiarity of s_i^2, known as the Herfindahl index, is that its distribution in studies of industrial concentration tends to be strongly skewed to the low end of the admissable range. Whether this is of any theoretical importance in our study is debatable. It depends on whether we believe that the cross-sectional distribution of our companies' degrees of diversification is truly skewed or that the skew is an artifact of the formula. Since nearly all of our subject firms are involved in five or six major product lines or fewer, the degree of skew observed may not be as severe as in the concentration studies that used the Herfindahl index. Nonetheless, since we make comparisons of indices across companies for relative degrees of diversification, it would seem useful to remove some of the skew by taking the log of s_i^2. Since the log of a fraction is less than zero, the resulting figure is multiplied by minus one to revert the index into a positive range.

Selected Bibliography

The literature on the subject of corporate and managerial goals is vast and reaches back in time at least to Adam Smith and *The Wealth of Nations*. This book owes a great deal to that literature in shaping the design and setting the context for the study. What follows is the author's selected list of the more recent books and articles from the academic and business literature as they relate to the particular issues of industrial financial goals in the United States.

Anthony, Robert N. "The Trouble with Profit Maximization." *Harvard Business Review* 38 (November–December 1960): 126–34.

Baumol, William J. *Business Behavior, Value and Growth*. rev. ed. New York: Harcourt, Brace & World, 1967.

Berle, Adolf A. and Means, Gardiner C. *The Modern Corporation and Private Property*. New York: Macmillan, 1932.

Bloom, Paul N. and Kotler, Philip. "Strategies for High Market Share Companies." *Harvard Business Review* 53 (November–December 1975): 63–72.

Chandler, Alfred D. *The Visible Hand: The Managerial Revolution in American Business*. Cambridge, MA: Harvard University Press, Belknap Press, 1977.

Cyert, Richard M. and March, James G. *A Behavioral Theory of the Firm*. Englewood Cliffs, NJ: Prentice-Hall, Inc., 1963.

Donaldson, Gordon. "Financial Goals: Management vs. Stockholders." *Harvard Business Review* 41 (May–June 1963): 116–29.

Fama, Eugene F. "Agency Problems and the Theory of the Firm." *Journal of Political Economy* 88 (1980): 288–307.

———. "Agency Problems and Residual Claims." *Journal of Law and Economics* 26 (1983): 327–49.

——— and Jensen, Michael C. "Separation of Ownership and Control." *Journal of Law and Economics* 26 (1983): 301–25.

Findlay, M. Chapman and Whitmore, G. A. "Beyond Shareholder Wealth Maximization." *Financial Management* 3 (1974): 25–35.

Fruhan, William E., Jr. *Financial Strategy: Studies in the Creation, Transfer, and Destruction of Shareholder Value.* Homewood, IL: Richard D. Irwin, Inc., 1979.

Higgins, Robert C. "How Much Growth Can a Firm Afford?" *Financial Management* 6 (1977): 7–16.

———. "Sustainable Growth Under Inflation." *Financial Management* 10 (1981): 36–40.

James, David R. and Soref, Michael. "Profit Constraints on Managerial Autonomy." *American Sociological Review* 46 (1981): 1–18.

Jensen, Michael C. and Meckling, William H. "Can the Corporation Survive?" *Financial Analysts Journal* 34 (1978): 31–37.

Mason, Edward S., ed. *The Corporation in Modern Society.* Cambridge, MA: Harvard University Press, 1959.

Meyers, Stewart C. "Finance Theory and Financial Strategy." *Interfaces*, in press.

Morris, Robin. "A Model of the *Managerial* Enterprise." *Quarterly Journal of Economics* 77 (1963): 185–209.

Murthy, K.R. Srinivasa. *Corporate Strategy and Top Executive Compensation.* Boston: Division of Research, Harvard Graduate School of Business Administration, 1977.

Seitz, Neil. "Shareholder Goals, Firm Goals and Firm Financing Decisions." *Financial Management* 11 (1982): 20–26.

Simon, Herbert A. "On the Concept of Organizational Goal." *Administrative Science Quarterly* 4 (1964): 1–22.

Stata, Ray and Madique, Modesto A. "Bonus System for Balanced Strategy." *Harvard Business Review* 58 (November–December 1980): 156–63.

Stonehill, Arthur, et al. "Financial Goals and Debt Ratio Determinants: A Survey of Practice in Five Countries." *Financial Management* 4 (1975): 27–41.

Treynor, Jack L. "The Financial Objective in the Widely Held Corporation." *Financial Analysts Journal* 37 (1981): 68–71.

Williamson, Oliver E. *The Economics of Discretionary Behavior: Managerial Objectives in a Theory of the Firm.* Englewood Cliffs, NJ: Prentice-Hall, Inc., 1964.

Wommack, William W. "The Board's Most Important Function." *Harvard Business Review* 57 (September–October 1979): 48–62.

Index

About the Author

Gordon Donaldson is Willard Prescott Smith Professor of Corporate Finance at the Graduate School of Business Administration, Harvard University. He has been on the Harvard faculty since 1955.

Dr. Donaldson has published a number of books and articles on the subject of corporate financial management for academic and business audiences.

Dr. Donaldson holds a B. Comm degree from the University of Manitoba, an M.A. in Economics from the University of Toronto, an M.B.A. from the University of Chicago and the Doctor of Commercial Science degree from Harvard University.